Criminology in a Hostile Environment

Also from Westphalia Press

westphaliapress.org

Criminology in a Hostile Environment

Volume 1, Number 1 of
International Journal on Criminology

Edited by
Alain Bauer

WESTPHALIA PRESS
An imprint of Policy Studies Organization

Criminology in a Hostile Environment
Volume 1, Number 1 of
International Journal on Criminology

Westphalia Press
An imprint of Policy Studies Organization
1527 New Hampshire Ave., N.W.
Washington, D.C. 20036
dgutierrezs@ipsonet.org

ISBN-13: 978-1935907381
ISBN-10: 1935907387

Cover design by Taillefer Long at Illuminated Stories:
www.illuminatedstories.com

Updated material and comments on this edition
can be found at the Westphalia Press website:
www.westphaliapress.org

Contents

Foreword

According to my colleagues at the University of Montreal, criminology "is the multidisciplinary study of the criminal phenomenon". It makes use of the humanities and social sciences (psychology, sociology, law, etc.) to understand the crime, the criminal, the victim, criminality, and society's reaction to crime.

Although everyone is aware of the criminal phenomenon, particularly through media exposure, the public understanding is often anecdotal and fragmentary. The criminologist looks beyond the headlines and takes a rigorously analytical and critical approach to criminality. He begins by analyzing the crime, before examining the type of intervention employed.

Criminology is also an applied discipline. The criminologist is trained, for example, to decide whether a prisoner should be granted conditional release, or to propose a strategy for tackling an explosion of vehicle theft in a parking lot. He thus develops risk prevention and risk management strategies that take into account the dynamics of crime and the ethical and political stakes surrounding it.

There are many journals covering criminal law, the criminal sciences and sociology, but very few international criminology reviews. We therefore aim to provide a space for open-minded dialogue, comparison, and criticism, which takes into account diverse approaches while avoiding sterile arguments about the nature of the discipline itself.

A crime is the unique combination of a perpetrator, a victim, and a set of circumstances. Its individual and quantitative analysis requires scientific methods and specific intellectual and technical abilities.

In *The Rules of Sociological Method* (1895), Emile Durkheim emphasizes that "[...] A number of acts can be observed, all with the external characteristic that once accomplished, they provoke this particular reaction from society known as punishment. We make of them a group *sui generis*, on which we impose a common rubric. We call any punished act a crime and make crime thus defined the focus of a dedicated science: criminology."

Such is the scope of this review.

Alain Bauer
French National Conservatory for Arts and Crafts, Paris
John Jay College of Criminal Justice. New York

The Art Of Criminology In A Hostile Environment

Alain Bauer

"The necessity of teaching criminology has been unanimously declared by all participants".

This unanimity is unsurprising, since criminology already has a long history as a scientific discipline. Following the works of Cesare Lombroso (1876), Enrico Ferri (1881), and Raffaele Garofalo (1885), it developed through numerous international congresses of criminal anthropology (Rome, 1885; Paris, 1889; Brussels, 1892; Geneva, 1896; Amsterdam, 1901; Turin, 1906; Cologne, 1911). This tradition continued with international congresses of criminology (Rome, 1938; Paris, 1950; London, 1955). However, all sciences are disposed to dissemination through organized teaching.

In fact, at the first International Congress of Criminal Anthropology, Tarde, supported by Enrico Ferri, proposed that students only be admitted to criminal law courses on condition that they first joined a prisoner patronage society and that they took part in weekly visits to prisons, either as groups or individually. In 1890, The Saint Petersburg International Penitentiary Congress expressed a wish "that a chair of penitentiary science be created in universities". A similar wish was formulated in 1895 by the Congress of the International Union of Penal Law held in Linz (Austria).

Since then, the idea has frequently been re-expressed. In London, in 1925, the Ninth International Penitentiary Congress affirmed that "legal training should be complemented by teaching of criminology". The Third International Congress of Penal Law, the First International Congress of Criminology and the Twelfth Penal and Penitentiary Congress subsequently expressed similar wishes. Finally, on December 17, 1952, the Meeting of Specialized Agencies and Non-Governmental Organizations Interested in the Prevention of Crime and the Treatment of Offenders, gathered in Geneva under the auspices of the UN, recommended:

1° that universities teach criminology and criminological subjects, according to local traditions, possibilities, and skills;

2° that this teaching be compulsory for those wishing to become judiciary or paralegal professionals;

3° that this teaching have recourse, more widely, to clinical exercises.

Thus, criminology teaching is thought to be necessary not only by criminologists themselves, but by all those involved in preventing crime and treating offenders. In fact, in most countries, there is a surge of opinion demanding a transformation of justice and penal administration. Police, magistrates, and prison staff everywhere feel the need for a change in their methods. However, in all countries, when they want to act on their good intentions, they find their efforts blocked by a severe or even total lack of norms and precedents. This situation has driven the most determined among them to undertake a difficult task, basing their efforts on practical experience alone, and faced every day with the proof that good will alone can change little. They therefore want scientific training in criminology to be put in place, to help them steer their efforts in the right direction.

They see this training as particularly indispensable since penal and penitentiary reform has created, alongside the traditional auxiliary staff within the penal service (such as medical examiners and psychiatric experts), a new breed of auxiliary staff including psychologists, social workers, and educators.[1] The resultant diversity of legal and paralegal staff makes cohesion difficult to achieve. In order to avoid fragmented work where no-one looks beyond their own domain, shared basic training is required.

Moreover, the evolution of viewpoints, institutions, and staff in the domain of crime prevention and offender treatment poses the question of a renewal of criminal law and procedure. Criminological factors must therefore be taken into account when constructing the rule of law. This means that conventional lawyers must be brought up to date with advances in criminology.

Finally, it should be remembered that beyond professional training for judges and their auxiliaries or for lawyers, criminological teaching is necessary to stimulate scientific research. This research cannot be successful without a constant effort to methodically classify the partial results obtained by individual researchers and integrate them into an overall science, where rigorous systematization allows them to be put in perspective, revealing their full significance. In this approach, training must separate what is confirmed from what is only thought to be true, break down watertight barriers in thinking, draw attention to urgent questions, and disseminate the latest research by various specialists in different countries.

These, in brief, are the arguments in favor of teaching criminology.

The agreement as to the need for criminological training would have been illusory without discussion regarding the definition of criminology itself.

This problem formed part of the investigation program and was presented to the different reporters. It was also largely addressed in the general introductory note written by one of our group and distributed at the London conference. Similarly, it was addressed at this conference by Mr. Benigno di Tullio, professor at the University of Rome and honorary president of the International Society for Criminology.

The vast majority of participants agreed on Enrico Ferri's conception of criminology as a "synthetic science" drawing upon criminal anthropology[1] and criminal sociology.

Today, as in the past, the objective of this synthetic science is to reduce criminality and, on the theoretical level that works towards this practical goal, to provide a complete study of the criminal and crime, the latter being viewed not as a judicial abstraction, but as a human action, as a fact of nature and society. The method employed in criminology is that of observation and experimentation, applied within the framework of a true social clinic.

It nevertheless goes without saying that in viewing criminology as a unitary and autonomous science that synthesizes results from clinics and experimentation, the participants at the London conference simply identified a direction—a path to follow. Clearly, this view of criminology supposes that the clinical, experimental approach is sufficiently integrated in practical institutions to allow serious research. The development of observation centers, penitentiary anthropology laboratories, and classification institutes is a prerequisite for the harmonious application of this approach. All were aware that when this condition is not fulfilled or only partially fulfilled, criminology must be content to remain a collection of sciences. It then embraces all those sciences linked to the criminal phenomenon. In these circumstances, it is more appropriate to speak of criminological sciences than of true criminology, since this term applies only to a synthesis of the constituent disciplines.

These two views: criminology as a collection of sciences and criminology as an autonomous science in itself are not mutually exclusive. They are in fact complementary. The social clinic of true criminology uses the methods and data of the fundamental disciplines together. Consequently, the teaching of criminology itself is an extension of, and not a replacement for, the teaching of criminological sciences.

It hardly needs emphasizing that the teaching of criminological subjects and criminology can be usefully complemented by that of related sciences such as legal forensics, scientific policing, and forensic psychology.[1] However, these disciplines should be clearly distinguished from the fundamental disciplines and from criminology itself. Although they study the criminal phenomenon, they do so only to establish the material facts and proof of the crime. They do not envisage scientific study of criminality or seek solutions, whereas this is the precise objective of criminology and the fundamental disciplines.

It is not necessary to insist further on the interest of teaching criminology and on its usefulness for training professionals, students, researchers, and teaching staff.

Essentially, this teaching, as defined above, concerns human criminal activity and aims to assist with the fight against the social ill that is crime. It can thus be perfectly incorporated into social sciences teaching.

When reading various national reports, it is impossible not to be struck by the multiplicity of structures involved in teaching criminology and by the diversity of statuses assigned to it.

One might be tempted to put these differences down to the pluralisms observed in the subject of criminology itself. These fundamental divergences undeniably have some influence at the institutional level. There is, in particular, what can be called an annexing tendency, in which old or traditional disciplines such as penal law consider criminology and the criminological sciences as auxiliary disciplines. This results in an attitude that makes a small space for these disciplines in a pre-established framework unfortunately not designed to accommodate them. The same trend can be seen outside of penal law, and the core disciplines are no exception. Although the situation varies between countries, sociology, psychology, biology, and penology all display an annexationist approach to criminology.

In fact, the principal factor in the multiplicity of structures for teaching criminology and in the diversity of statuses attributed to it is the variation in the organization of university studies between countries. The contrast is typically made between continental European and Anglo-Saxon universities.

Cambridge University professor M. C. W. Guillebaud emphasized these differences in his remarkable general report on the teaching of economic sciences, which forms the opening to the study of these disciplines in this collection. We will not dwell on the matter here, but it should be noted that his observations are equally applicable to criminology.

These differences in the "structure, organization and hierarchy" of qualifications between Anglo-Saxon and continental universities have repercussions for university teaching of criminology. The Anglo-Saxon system is less homogeneous than the continental European system, and the United Kingdom system differs from that of the United States (which displays characteristics of both systems). Any brief, general comment on these differences risks being misleading. Instead, the most important differences for criminology are addressed in the various sections of this report. It is nevertheless possible to make the following preliminary observations:

1. An important difference impacting on the treatment of criminology is that between state and private universities. The tight state control over continental universities and the resultant high uniformity in structure and organization makes for greater uniformity in university teaching of criminology in continental Europe than in the UK. Conversely, the autonomy of British private universities, despite the financial aid they receive, allows for greater diversity in exams, programs, and degrees. This naturally creates variation

between universities in terms of the importance given to criminology, the number of hours devoted to the subject, the breadth of the topics covered, and the level to which it is taught.

The second consequence of this difference results from it being easier for universities with highly state-controlled administration to provide criminology training for police officers and for penal, probation,[1] or correctional staff. With looser ties between the State and universities, as seen in the UK, the State tends to organize criminological teaching outside of universities for police and correctional staff. This key difference is clearly visible in the details about training for civil servants found in national reports. Remarkably, there are even differences between Anglo-Saxon countries: The United Kingdom has only private and independent universities, whereas the United States has a mix of state and private universities, so some training colleges for policing and correctional staff are attached to universities, while many others are independent.

2. In general (although wide variation within the system makes generalizations impossible), the Anglo-Saxon system gives less attention to the subjects often united under the umbrella of criminology (legal forensics, scientific policing, and forensic psychology). Yet this does not imply any disaffection for these subjects. They are simply treated as specialisms and taught accordingly, within lessons devoted to the core disciplines, or in specialist courses offered by institutes or other educational establishments (including teaching organized by the services concerned, for example the police).

3. Another important difference arises from the teaching of sociology being more developed in U.S. universities and, to a lesser degree, in UK universities, than in continental Europe. It also arises from the fact that sociology itself has taken a great interest in criminology. This phenomenon has influenced the teaching and direction of criminology, even outside of universities. The discipline is therefore widely taught in sociology departments in the United States and United Kingdom, whereas departments in continental Europe emphasize the links between criminology and law.

Nevertheless, although specializations are not taught when criminology is taught at a general, elementary level, specialist subjects such as psychiatry and legal forensics are taught as part of the core disciplines in both systems.

4. The hierarchy of university qualifications differs widely between the two systems, but this difference is more a matter of words than of knowledge levels. Nevertheless, Mr. Guillebaud's comments are perfectly applicable to criminology.

5. Many criminology courses exist outside of universities in the United Kingdom and the United States. This complex organization of teaching and the freedom given to educational establishments constitute the two most striking characteristics of the Anglo-Saxon system. These courses either demonstrate the universities' interest in allowing students to audit courses, or are a response to the professional needs of particular groups.

The in-service training courses for probation officers, the preparatory courses for certain police officer grades, and the courses organized in psychiatric clinics for correctional case workers are all examples of the latter scenario.

The later sections of this report provide greater detail on this complex teaching structure outside of universities. In general, it can be said that this characteristic of the Anglo-Saxon system aims to provide training that is better adapted to the needs of the professional environment.

6. A further difference between the two systems is that the United Kingdom and United States have highly developed training in social work, with a wide variety of qualifications, diplomas, and certifications. This is particularly visible in criminology teaching in the UK, where probation officers follow a two-year, full-time university

course in order to obtain a social science diploma, before undertaking more specialist training at the Home Office.

In both countries, many of these courses are not directly linked to criminology, despite having some relationship to it. This trend generally results in improved professional training, producing greater professional competence among the clinical criminologists that are social workers and probation officers.

7. The two systems are deeply entrenched and almost incomparably different. Nevertheless, in both systems, teaching of a multidisciplinary science such as criminology could benefit from the creation of university criminology institutes (naturally, with the appropriate adaptations for each system). This suggestion applies to the Anglo-Saxon as well as the continental system. However, given the current situation in Anglo-Saxon countries, it would have been more logical to distinguish between the criminology taught "inside" and "outside" universities rather than that taught "inside" and "outside" criminology institutes. This latter classification has nevertheless been retained here to facilitate comparison between various national datasets.

By using this division and by means of this study, we hope to emphasize that each system could benefit from drawing more than they have done so far upon study of the other's respective advantages.

It seems that such study could lead to a greater number of reforms than have been made to date. With this in mind, international exchange of knowledge and experts, encouraged by the International Society for Criminology, can only be beneficial.

Criminology institutes are proposing to unite teaching of criminology, the criminological sciences, and sometimes also criminal law within a single institution. Their organization varies widely: they may be public or private, taking the form of institutes or universities.

As regards their public or private nature, there is quite a clear distinction between Anglo-Saxon institutes and continental European institutes.

Anglo-Saxon institutes are usually private. This is how the Institute for the Study and Treatment of Delinquency, founded in London as a private company in 1931 and initially an open clinic for examining delinquents of all ages, later became an evening school dedicated to social studies, with the fourth year focusing on criminology (these courses depended on the Extra-Mural Department of the University of London and thus on the institution's extension learning service).[1] In the United States, where higher education establishments are too numerous and too diverse for any generalization to be made, it is possible to single out professional development institutes, which target professionals and depend on both the university and the State. One example is the Institute of Correctional Administration, created under the auspices of the General Studies College of George Washington University, which acts as a professional development centre for prison and probation service staff.

Although the institute model is not very developed in Anglo-Saxon countries,[3] the same cannot be said of continental countries, where institutes are generally (but not always) public. This is the case in Austria (the Vienna and Graz institutes), Belgium (the criminology departments of the State universities of Ghent and Liège), Brazil (the institute of the Federal District University), France (the Paris and provincial institutes), Italy (the Rome institute), Turkey (the Istanbul and Ankara institutes), and Yugoslavia (the Sarajevo, Ljubljana and Belgrade institutes). All of these are public institutes.

Along with these institutes, the criminology department of the Free University of Leuven and the criminological sciences department of the Free University of Brussels should be mentioned. These are private, but like the institutes listed above, they are university establishments.

The only organized institute existing outside of a university in the continental European countries is the School of Criminology and Technical Policing of the Belgian Ministry of Justice, which is to some extent comparable to American professional development institutes.

Almost all of the university institutes are attached to law faculties, with the sole exception of the Stockholm Institute, which since 1947 has been a university institute, while remaining privately funded.

This attachment to law faculties has certain consequences. In Paris, the Institute of Criminology is under the scientific direction of the law faculty, the head of its administrative council is the dean of the law faculty, and the director and associate director must be members of the current criminal law teaching body. In Rome, the director is the professor of penal law. In Ljubljana, the director is elected by the law faculty from among its teachers.

Such measures are significant and reveal a lingering juridical imperialism belonging to the old view of criminology as an auxiliary science annexed to or complementing criminal law. One might legitimately wonder whether this juridical preeminence, which once corresponded to a certain historical state of affairs, is now outdated. Criminology supposes a multidisciplinary approach to the individual case and, to judge by the continental countries, its core disciplines belong to the medical and humanities faculties.

In such conditions, it appears that the exclusive attachment of criminology institutes to law faculties might provoke criticisms or reservations from various members of the criminological team. It would therefore be appropriate to bring teaching of criminology within institutes onto neutral grounds, with the "university institute" model seeming preferable to that of "institute attached to the law faculty".

Outside of criminology institutes, the subject is taught in university faculties and establishments linked to scientific research or professional training.[1]

In the Anglo-Saxon countries, criminology is widely taught in university faculties. In the UK, it is linked to the development of social science teaching in universities. The University of London, the London School of Economics (not forgetting the Institute of Psychiatry), and the social sciences faculty at Oxford University seem to have been at the forefront of the movement, followed by numerous universities. At Cambridge, however, criminology is taught within the criminal science department of the law faculties. Elsewhere, it is part of the psychology department (Aberdeen) or the psychological medicine department (Durham).

In the United States, of the 30 most important universities offering graduate training, only five do not teach criminology. In addition to this, 607 colleges (65% of American colleges) offer undergraduate courses in sociology, and criminology is one of the most popular subjects in these courses. This teaching is mostly provided by the sociology or sociology and anthropology departments. Criminology sometimes constitutes a specialist subdivision of the social sciences, while the University of California has a separate criminology department.

In the Anglo-Saxon countries, criminology, in the form of criminal sociology, has thus become closely integrated into the social sciences and sociology departments. This is not the case in continental European countries. Courses in many different faculties undoubtedly evoke "criminological" problems in passing (psychology and sociology courses within humanities departments, legal forensics and psychiatry courses in medical faculties, or criminal law courses in law faculties). However, core disciplines of criminology are rarely offered individually, exceptions including criminal anthropology in Italy, criminal psychology at the Catholic University in Milan, and forensic psychiatry at Stockholm University. However, many law faculties offer basic teaching more or less complementary to criminal law, under the name "criminology". For now, it is sufficient to note the existence of such teaching, as seen at Innsbruck in Austria, at Rio de Janeiro and São Paulo in Brazil, and at Ankara and Istanbul in Turkey. In France, a recent reform introduced a semester of penal law and criminology in the second year of undergraduate law degrees.

Comparable to this university teaching is that provided in certain establishments in connection with scientific research. These establishments and the kinds of teaching they offer are essentially diverse. Sometimes, the research centre complements university teaching, as is the case in London, Oxford, and Cambridge. Similarly, in Belgium, the René Marcq Center at the Free University of Brussels provides criminological training for researchers. In France, the School for Advanced Studies provides criminal sociology teaching for researchers and the School of Anthropology (a private institution founded by Broca) offers a criminology course.

Most of the countries studied also offer professional training courses in connection with universities or the various relevant institutions. This model has allowed the University of London and numerous other British universities to organize "extension" teaching for police and social workers. The Home Office and Scottish Home Department take responsibility for training civil servants working in probation, the police service, the prison service, borstal houses, and approved schools. In Belgium, criminology is taught in nursing and social service schools. France has a school for prison staff and schools for police and educators, organized by the relevant administrative bodies and teaching rudimentary criminology. This is also the case in Italy, which has a graduate scientific policing school, as well as a school and professional development courses for social workers. In the United States, teaching for police and penitentiary staff takes place in universities, usually in separate divisions (such as the Berkeley school in California).

Teaching is also provided for social workers. Finally, Sweden has an institute for social assistants in Gëteborg, offering forensic psychiatry and juvenile criminology courses.

This overview of the structure and status of criminology teaching reveals great disparity. Clearly, this disparity is to some extent an inevitable result of the way things are. However, although it cannot be entirely avoided, it could at least be limited if the model of the university criminology institute already suggested above could be accompanied by centralization and effective coordination of teaching for criminology and the criminological sciences.

The organization of criminology and criminological science teaching presents numerous problems: The conditions for admission, the cost of studies, the number of students, the teaching cycle (duration of studies, exams, and qualifications) and employment prospects.

The access conditions for criminology and criminological science teaching display similar disparity to the structure and status of this teaching.

In the case of criminology institutes, we know that Anglo-Saxon institutes are highly specialist centers. As written by one of our group, their function is the "multidisciplinary teaching of criminology to people who are already highly trained in one of the related sciences". The program at the Institute for the Treatment and the Study of Delinquency in London includes courses aimed at specialists, while also providing for the learning needs of non-specialists. In the United States, prior professional selection is used in admission procedures for the specialist institutes, because of the limited number of places. This explains why the model is one of professional development schools.[1] In Belgium, the

School of Criminology and Technical Policing of the Ministry of Justice is reserved for magistrates, lawyers, university graduates, and those with specialist knowledge.

In continental European criminology institutes attached to law faculties, there are two models for entry conditions. In the first, institute courses in criminology, the criminological sciences and related sciences form an ensemble and must all be studied together. Criminology teaching is consequently independent of the law program. It is an additional course with particular entry requirements. In the second model, however, courses at the criminology institute do not form an ensemble. Law students simply have to follow one of the courses during their studies.

When teaching at a criminology institute is compulsory and complementary, proof of prior scientific training is an admission requirement. The Leuven criminology school in Belgium accepts applicants holding an "applicant" university degree and medical students having successfully completed the second year, which serves as an "application" test in the natural and medical sciences. Similar conditions apply in Brussels, Ghent, and Liège. In Paris, only students with at least a Bachelors in law or holding a certificate of legal competence are admitted, together with students in the humanities, science, or medicine. In Rome, graduates in law, economy, commerce, or the political and social sciences, and medical doctors or surgeons, as well as those holding a degree from another university, can register. In Turkey and Yugoslavia, admission depends on academic and professional qualifications.

It can thus be seen that when a criminology institute provides compulsory or additional teaching, the entry conditions range from those applied to ordinary higher education applicants (as in Belgium), to conditions similar to those required by Anglo-Saxon style professional development institutes (as in Rome, Turkey, and Yugoslavia), with a variety of intermediary situations (as in Paris). The same does not apply when one of the programs is compulsory for law students (Vienna, Graz): They must take two hours of criminology per week for one semester. It should also be noted that students in other faculties can attend the institute's courses. Auditing is also allowed on these courses.

Given these admission requirements, it is remarkable that no establishment asks applicants to take a preparatory course teaching the basics of biology, psychology, and sociology—notions without which it would seemingly be very difficult to follow anything more than a rudimentary course. General or specialist university qualifications or even professional experience in particular areas cannot be a substitute for the rational acquisition of this basic knowledge.

Criminological teaching outside of institutes is less problematic in terms of entry conditions. In the UK, where criminology is most often taught as a branch of the social sciences, it is obviously the entry conditions for these studies that count. Similarly, in the United States, all sociology or social administration students have the opportunity to follow the general criminology modules in universities. In the Anglo-Saxon countries, the criminological sciences are also taught outside of sociology departments, as a part of the general teaching of the other core disciplines. In continental Europe, specialized teaching in the core disciplines (criminal anthropology, forensic psychology, forensic psychology), where it exists, takes place within the framework of corresponding studies in medicine and psychology. Notions of criminology within or linked to criminal law are reserved for law students. The same applies for humanities or medical students, when criminological notions are evoked in relation to other courses in their programs (such as psychology, sociology, psychiatry, or forensics)."

The text above is plagiarized. The words do not belong to the person citing them. It is not a modern text. It dates back to 1956 and was written by Denis Carroll and Jean Pinatel for the UNESCO Congress on Criminology. The Congress took place in Paris. Criminology developed everywhere...everywhere except France.

In fact, since the 1950s, academic pressures have never stopped pitching disciplinary monopolies against criminology's fight to be recognized as a scientific discipline. Criminology is essentially just one in a long line of disciplines defending its turf as part of a struggle for recognition. Yet these other struggles have been rapidly forgotten. In fact, criminology is not the only discipline to have suffered. Before it, the oriental languages (under Francis I of France), the sciences and technologies, economy and management (during the French Revolution), political science (during the Second Empire) and many other disciplines including penal law and journalism were not accepted by the old Sorbonne. The situation is, unfortunately, nothing new.

One might think that Emile Durkheim himself would have been able to resolve this famous controversy: "[...] A number of acts can be observed, all with the external characteristic that once accomplished, they provoke this particular reaction from society known as punishment. We make of them a group sui generis, on which we impose a common rubric. We call any punished act a crime, thus making crime the focus of a dedicated science: Criminology". *The rules of sociological method* (*Les règles de la méthode sociologique,* 1895), PUF, Quadrige, 1981, 35.

Others have also made determined and equally worthy efforts to define criminology: Jacques Léaute, in *Criminology and penitentiary law* (*Criminologie et science pénitentiaire*, P.U.F., 1972), states that "The aim of criminology is the scientific study of the whole criminal phenomenon".

Stefani, Gaston, Georges Levasseur and R. Jambu-Merlin, *Criminology and penitentiary law* (*Criminologie et science pénitentiaire*, Fifth Edition, 1982) state that "The criminological sciences are those that study delinquency in order to look for its causes, its origins, its processes and consequences".

Gassin, Raymond. *Criminology* (*Criminologie*, Précis Dalloz, Sixth Edition, 2007) defines it as "[...] the science that studies the factors and processes of criminal action and which determines, using knowledge of these factors and processes, the best means of combat to contain and if possible reduce this social ill".

Ellenberger. *Criminology past and present* (*Criminologie du passé et du present*, 1966) asserts that "Alongside the general sciences, criminology belongs to the complex sciences, and like them it is recognizable by the following characteristics:

1. [It is] located at a crossroads with sciences from which [...] it remains separate, but to which it is related [...];

2. It is not purely theoretical, and is given meaning only by its practical application [...];

3. It is neither entirely general nor entirely specific, but rather it constantly moves back and forth from general to specific, specific to general [...];

4. It works not only with scientific concepts but also with concepts expressing value judgments [...];

5. It is characterized by an independent ethical goal: To prevent crime, rather than have to punish it. If punishment is necessary, the minimum effective punishment should be used, and reeducation should be combined with the punishment [...]"

Cario, Robert. *Introduction to the criminal sciences* (*Introduction aux sciences criminelles*, Sixth Editon, 2008, 260) affirms that "criminology can be defined as a multidisciplinary science whose objective is the global and integrated analysis of the social phenomenon caused by criminal actions, in their origins and their dynamics, in their individual and social dimensions, from the viewpoint of the perpetrator as well as that of the victim, for goals of prevention and treatment".

One might believe that this avalanche would have been enough to stem the sociolatry whose denial of reality constituted at once its charm, its difference and its fundamentalism, particularly in France… and only in France…

For, as discussed with the professors Villerbu, Herzog Evans, and Cario in a recent tribune,[1] a discipline is above all a political fact whose scientific aim must integrate recognition in order to re-establish its goals. The autonomy of penal law, the birth of the criminal sciences, the recognition of the very notion of criminal policies had to be argued politically, as did the free practice of university teaching of clinical psychology or of sociology. The fact that contemporary criminal lawyers have chosen to write a treatise on penal law and criminology[2] clearly shows that the two cannot be thought of as the same discipline, just as criminology cannot be reduced to the criminal sciences, even if they are accompanied by sociological considerations and psychological or psychiatric humanism.[3]

Although criminology is taught in France, it has no official university recognition, in that there is no qualification for it. It can only be an add-on whose disciplinary avatars are weak. It therefore takes refuge at worst in private institutions, at best in university degrees or interuniversity degrees. The number of these has continued to rise, reaching 130 in 2010. According to the Villerbu Report, this explains the words used by members of the National Criminology Conference[4] in November 2009 to designate both studies of criminology and those that benefited from it: "Homeless" and "paperless". However, the media constantly continues to promote criminological information that is often partial, sometimes in both senses of the word. The *scoop* is prioritized over educational value.[5] It should also be emphasized that criminological thought forms part of the teaching of over 110 university academics and interests many practical stakeholders, despite the fact that work in criminology severely lacks visibility.

The French paradox arises from these points: since emerging at the end of the nineteenth century at the crossroads between four recognized disciplines (medicine, legal, psychiatry/mental health, law, sociology), criminology remained an accessory to penal law, which is simply a long-ignored component of private law. Its legitimacy as an academic and social discipline comes in a context of institutional deficiency. It seems that systematic or systemic analysis is not appropriate for studying the criminal phenomenon: criminology tends to rely on texts, doctrine, case-law,[6] or the multiple theories in the

---

[1] "La criminologie est elle une science," *Cahiers Français*, January 2013.

[2] G. Stefani and G. Levasseur, *Droit pénal général et criminologie* (Paris: Dalloz, 1957); J. Léauté and R. Vouin, *Droit pénal et criminologie* (Thémis, Paris: PUF, 1956). See also P. Bouzat and J. Pinatel. *Traité de droit pénal et de criminologie* (Paris: Dalloz, 1970).

[3] When dealing with the relationship of crime (a judicial formulation) to criminal (the person responsible for the crime), these take the names of criminal psychology, criminal psychiatry, and criminal sociology.

[4] L. Villerbu, Report by the Minister of Higher Education and Research, on the Feasibility, Creation and Development of Criminology Studies, Research and Training (*Rapport Villerbu*). Presented at the French National Criminology Conference, 2010.

[5] No news item would be complete without an interview from a self-proclaimed criminologist.

[6] See B. Bouloc, *Pénologie* (Paris: Précis Dalloz, 1991).

humanities and the social, economic, or political sciences. When the observations are practical, we see a return to their disciplinary origin, even if this is highly disputed: Can psychiatry really be a way of understanding all criminal behavior? Does sociology have all the answers? Can psychology be sure of the origin of criminal ideas and acts, of the victim's position etc, when their fragmentation necessitates a selective vision if totalitarianism is to be avoided?[7]

Because criminology in France is seen as a specialism and not as a discipline, the effects of norms and changes to norms give little occasion for study that might enrich the perspectives of public policies for the territory or the town in question. The discipline thus gives little attention to collective criminality (organized crime and terrorism), to transnational criminality (cartels and mafias), to forms of criminality attributable to the state of the modern world (the "dark side" of globalization), or to the development of criminal networks with the opening up of markets, the development of new technologies and new forms of consumerism.

The National Criminology Conference, which benefited from the presence of field professionals and analyzed observations by representatives of diverse origins and opinions in an attempt to end the clandestine practices of members and partial institutions,[8] submitted its conclusions in July 2011. The report only began to pose problems for some when, after a few reformulations and conditions, it came to creating a criminology department. The decree creating such a department within the National Council of Universities, as well as the educational and research structures to accompany it, was published in the official journal of March 15, 2012. It was repealed in August of the same year, due to a change in the political majority.

France's National Criminology Conference aimed to make global and integrated research in the undergraduate, masters, and doctoral systems possible[9] and to guarantee democratic access for all (this is not currently the situation in private or even public university programs). Initial, specialized, or ongoing training for teachers, researchers, and professionals in the penal system or generally involved in dealing with crimes committed or suffered would ideally guarantee scientific content based on an ethic of independence and freedom of the universities, as required by the traditional deontology of university personnel and by the pedagogical imperatives that they follow. In the words of Edgar Morin and Stéphane Hessel, these considerations are typical "of a love of the knowledge delivered and the people that it is delivered to".[10]

There are three easily identifiable levels of criminological intervention. The first is prevention programs for all forms of vulnerability, corresponding to various professions, which aim to reduce the risk factors affecting vulnerable children and adolescents. These programs aim to strengthen protection measures and assist harmonious (re)integration. The second, when prevention fails, is intervention throughout the penal process by professionals with critical knowledge based on experience and exposure to research. Their knowledge areas range from the effects of violent acts to those of past violence, as

---

[7] "Science ou justice. Les savants, l'ordre et la loi" *Autrement* 145 (1994), Série Mutations/sciences en société.

[8] The price of these clandestine practices is high: the partisans of existing disciplines ensure that many criminology teaching jobs go to pre-selected or inside candidates, and many teachers expressing an interest in criminology are passed over for promotion.

[9] L. Villerbu, *Rapport Villerbu*, 39-62.

[10] E. Morin and S. Hessel. *Le chemin de l'espérance* (Paris: Fayard, 2011), 20-21.

seen in secondary victimization.[11] The third consists of ways of dealing with crime and its perpetrators, which result, as far as possible, in re-cognition. Strengthening of skills among those who deal with condemned criminals would encourage criminals to "desist"[12] (stop reoffending). These skills go beyond the social, economic, or psychological factors of reinsertion that are traditionally seen as factors in ending delinquency. Developments of this kind have led to remarkable creations of "therapeutic jurisprudence"[13] in the United States, or of jurisdictions that resolve the problem at hand.

However, this kind of intervention will remain a pious wish unless independent, scientific, regular, and sustained solutions are applied.

There have been numerous criticisms of this new division of criminology. Although "contestation is a necessary condition for renewal of a science",[14] objections are all too often based on unfounded common opinion and illegitimate reductionism. Security-based ideology,[15] personal criticisms[16] and worries about the instrumentalization of universities[17] discredit the objections, unless it is to be considered that scientific disciplines, autonomous or otherwise, necessarily belong to current political thought, even if their applications are universal.

We should expect criminology to address the suffering of victims in a practical, humane, restorative, and therapeutic manner, as well as a scientifically enlightened and well-founded one. Those adhering to certain currents of thought are generally uncomfortable with victims,[18] since they focus—as we all must also do—on the

---

[11] Secondary victimization is when a person re-lives their trauma upon the occurrence of a new event that may or may not be linked to the initial trauma.

[12] See for example F. McNeill, P. Raynor, and C. Trotter *Offender Supervision: New Directions in Theory, Research and Practice* (Willan Publishing, 2010).

[13] M. Herzog-Evans, "Révolutionner la pratique judiciaire. S'inspirer de l'inventivité américaine," *Recueil Dalloz* (2011): 3016-3022.

[14] G. Kellens, "Interactionnisme versus personnalité criminelle," *Les grandes tendances de la criminologie contemporaine* (Proceedings of the 7th International Criminology Congress of Belgrade, 1973). Institut des recherches criminologiques et sociales, Vol. 1, 1980, 118-128.

[15] V.N. Brafman and I. Rey-Lefebvre. "La criminologie érigée en discipline autonome,, *Le Monde*, March 14, 2012; H. Damien, "La criminologie: nouvelle discipline universitaire en France," *France Soir*, March 17, 2012; Motion carried on March 21, 2012 by the permanent Commission of the National Council of Universities (CPCNU); H. Tassel, "La criminologie à l'université? Fuite en avant, imposture scientifique et désinvolture...," March 23, 2012. http://humanite.fr; Collective (L. Mucchielli, O. Nay, X. Pin, and D. Zagury), "La 'criminologie' entre succès médiatique et rejet universitaire," *Le Monde*, March 29, 2012; "Création d'une Section du CNU 'criminologie': non à la Section 'Guéant'," April 4, 2012. http://ferc-sup.cgt.fr.

[16] See L. Mucchielli "Une 'nouvelle criminologie française'. Pour qui et pour quoi?" *Revue de Science criminelle et de droit pénal comparé*, 2008–2004, 795-803; L. Mucchielli "Vers une criminologie d'État en France? Institutions, acteurs et doctrines d'une nouvelle science policière," *Politix* 2010-23-89, 195-214; "La 'criminology' en France et ses arrière-plans idéologiques," March 20, 2011. http://laurent.mucchielli.org; Ruling creating a criminology section published in the *Journal Officiel*, March 15, 2012. http://vousnousils.fr).

[17] See "Non à la 75è section". http://petition24.net; "Déclaration des présidents du Conseil scientifique et du Conseil des formations du CNAM," April 24, 2012; V. Gautron, L. Leturmy, C. Mouhanna, and L. Mucchielli. "Criminologie en France (suite): pour un moratoire total sur les projets actuels," http://laurent.mucchielli.org.

[18] Relevant here is the experience described in D. Lemarchal, "La victime et son autre," *Ajpénal* (2008): 349-351.

criminals. Victims are therefore seen as an obstacle to dealing with delinquents.[19] Does this mean that these researchers are incapable of feeling equal empathy for the delinquents and the victims, or is it because consideration of victims casts doubt on the current penal process? It should be noted that even the first criminologists, albeit incidentally, drew attention in their work to the inevitable consideration of the victim within the penal response to the criminal act. Thus, founders of criminology such as Enrico Ferri and Raffaele Garofalo thought that remedying the harm to victims of criminal acts was a necessary objective of punishment.

These considerations led France's National Criminology Conference to state that *"criminology is 'the scientific study of the criminal phenomenon and the responses that are applied or could be applied by society', taking into account penal flaws, deviations and contraventions. It has a triple objective: Prevention, control and treatment. Current public policy is used to provide a context and perspective for study. Each of the three objectives gives rise to its own research path and content: Prevention may be primary, secondary or tertiary; control involves identifying, characterizing and stopping the criminal and the consequences of crime (the procedures, the forensic, psychiatric and psychological examinations, the alternatives to prosecution); treatment poses questions regarding the rights of parties, help for victims, reintegration or rehabilitation, restorative responses, compensation or mediation. These research paths require experienced and "certified" specialists.*

One hundred and twenty-eight years after Durkheim, 57 years after the Paris Congress, with criminology now also taught in France (officially at the National Conservatory Arts and Crafts only), it is becoming an emerging discipline. It no longer needs scientific justification or concrete acknowledgement. What it needs now is to rally society.

About the Author
Alain Bauer serves as Professor of Criminology at the French National Conservatory for Arts and Crafts (Paris) and as a Senior Research Fellow at the John Jay College of Criminal Justice (New York) and the University of Law and Political Science of China (Beijing).

---

[19] R. Cario. "Qui a peur des victimes," *Ajpénal* (2004): 434-437.

Restorative Justice: The Dual Recognition of Crime Victims and Offenders

Robert Cario

Restorative justice emerged in the English-speaking world in the 1970s,[1] and since the 1980s has gradually developed in Continental Europe to varying degrees. Apart from a few rare measures (rare in their nature and their application), it has been oddly slow to take hold in France. Yet with the traditional criminal justice system afflicted by crisis in recent years, it is full of promise.[2] Despite this obvious crisis of the purely punitive approach to criminal justice, we should not be blind to the considerable progress achieved since the Enlightenment and given concrete expression in the recent advent of human rights. The current system aims to respect the rights of protagonists in a conflict by ensuring the rule of law (particularly the principles of legality, equality, and due process) and protection of individuals (essentially the principles of dignity, protection of victims, and the presumption of innocence). Criminal proceedings have become increasingly fair (due to the principles of independence and impartiality of the judiciary, of respect for the right to defense, of equality of arms, and of professionalism) and effective (with the principles of proportionality and a swift trial). Similarly, consideration of the protagonists' personalities (offenders, victims, and families) and of their respective environments, and a concern for their expectations and needs, have led to the provision of legal, psychological, and social support and monitoring programs from the moment the offense is committed until they are reintegrated into society as fully and harmoniously as possible. More recently, a growing awareness of the complementary potentialities of restorative justice measures holds great promise for the enhancement of the criminal justice system.

1. The crisis of the contemporary penal system and the emergence of restorative justice

The fact remains that today, the penal machine continues to run blind: it defines neither the crime, nor the punishment, nor the victim. Far from being specific to the French system, similar liberties are taken with the very object of the justice system's *raison d'être* in most countries in the world. This has serious consequences, giving free rein to all sorts of interpretations and removing any possibility of evaluating the objectives sought. Yet each of these key concepts of criminal justice may be given an overall definition, without too much trouble; except, that is, that by the same token this would explicitly acknowledge the functional deficiencies and structural shortcomings of the current system. *Crime*, in the general sense of penology, is manifest in the infringement of a value considered fundamental for the human, social, and cultural sustainability of the group within which the conflict emerged. This is simply a logical and coherent application of the principles of justice and of utility, which alone can serve to

---

[1]. H. Zehr, *Changing Lenses: A New Focus for Crime and Justice* (Herald Press, 1990); H. Zehr, *La justice restaurative. Pour sortir des impasses de la logique punitive* (Labor et Fides, 2012).

[2]. R. Cario, *La justice restaurative. Principes et promesses*, L'Harmattan, Paris, Coll. Sciences criminelles, Second Edition, 2010; D. Salas, *La justice dévoyée. Critique des utopies sécuritaires* (Paris: Les Arènes, 2012).

legitimate and implement the criminalization of prohibited acts and/or behaviors. The *victim* therefore appears just as logically to be a person who has been harmed. Their suffering must be personal, genuine, socially recognized as unacceptable, and liable to justify some action being taken in favor of the individual concerned. This may include, as appropriate, the naming of the crime or the event, medical treatment or psychotherapy, psychological or social support, and/or compensation. In this notional context, the *penalty* (in the broad sense of sentences and security measures) for the infringement of essential social values resulting in harm being caused to a victim or victims consists in a punishment (incompatible with any form of humiliation) being inflicted by the legal authority of the group concerned or its representatives on anyone found criminally responsible. It is oriented towards the social rehabilitation of the person concerned and, more generally, towards restoring social harmony.[3]

The crisis of the modern correctional system can easily be illustrated by a few examples of punitive legal measures and practices. The increase in criminal legislation—which is swelling at an exorbitant rate[4]—is so inflated that corresponding litigation cannot be usefully processed. And yet "where there is inflation, there is depreciation: when the law is long-winded, citizens stop paying attention".[5] The rate of dismissal of complaints, denunciations, and reports by the criminal investigation department confirms this categorically: eight cases out of 10. Individual deterrence through criminal prohibition is scarcely more effective. Of the 15,000 officially registered prohibited acts (there are certainly many more, closer to 30,000, scattered throughout a range of documents of variable scope), criminal jurisdictions appear to use only 200 offenses, of which 60, moreover, account for 90% of convictions.[6] Widespread decriminalization is therefore urgently required and liable to return 80% of the conflicts which today are all too easily established as offenses to their original dispute status.

The social reaction to crime, although often disproportionate to the seriousness of the offenses committed (heavily concentrated around property crime), is resolutely harsh, with "prison having colonized punishment".[7] Yet the significant rise in recent decades of a strategy of "prisonization"[8] (over 100,000 years of prison sentences handed out in 2008)[9] despite endemic prison overcrowding (66,915 prisoners incarcerated on June 1, 2012, for 57,127 prison beds),[10] the doubling of the average length of sentences for low-

---

[3]. For more on these points, see Cario, La Justice restaurative; R. Cario, *Introduction aux sciences criminelles. Pour une approche globale et intégrée du phénomène criminel*, Vol. 4, Sixth Edition, 2008, 177etseq.; R. Cario, *De l'effraction du lien intersubjectif à la restauration sociale*, Vol. 2-1, Fourth Edition, 2012, forthcoming.

[4]. J. Carbonnier, *Droit et passion du droit sous la Vè République*, Flammarion, 1997, 107 et seq. The author further stresses that "the trouble with the Penal Code appears to come more from an impression of perpetual propagation" [translated from French, "avec le Code pénal, le trouble procéderait plutôt d'une impression d'accouchement perpetual"], 136.

[5]. Conseil d'Etat, *Rapport public 1991*, La Documentation Française, 1992-43, Coll. Etudes et documents, 20 [translated from French, "qui dit inflation dit dévalorisation: quand le droit bavarde, le citoyen ne lui prête plus qu'une oreille distraite"].

[6]. Y. Charpenel, *Les rendez-vous de la politique pénale. Concilier devoir de justice et exigence de sécurité*, A. Colin, Coll. Sociétales, 2006, 57.

[7]. R. Merle and A. Vitu, *Traité de droit criminel. Problèmes généraux de la science criminelle*, Tome 1, *Droit pénal général*, Editions Cujas, Seventh Edition. 1997, 900, citing M. Foucault.

[8]. G. Kellens, *Punir. Pénologie et droit des sanctions pénales*, 2000, Liège: Editions juridiques de l'Université de Liège, 76 et seq. and ref. cited.

[9]. P. Tournier, in *Arpenter le champ pénal*, 2010-175, arpenter-champ-penal.blogspot.com

[10]. Tournier, *Arpenter le Champ Pénal*, pierre-victortournier.blogspot.com.

to mid-level felony, the increase in custodial sentences of between five and 10 years, and the staggering drop in probation measures and alternative sanctions have had no effect on the volume of infringements.[11] Similarly, the average rate of recidivism, including recidivism by released prisoners, is abnormally high, except—and this is essential to note—for recidivism in serious, violent crime, which remains exceptional.[12] And what should be made of the increasingly frequent incarceration of individuals who were mentally incapacitated at the time of the offense?

The morphology of criminal activity does not justify such severity. A vast majority of offenses are misdemeanors to mid-level felonies involving commonplace property crime, consistent perhaps with the importance placed on the possession of goods and property in our excessively consumerist society.[13] The offenders come in large part from underprivileged social groups stricken by various types of poverty.[14] In such conditions, very close attention must be paid to the shape of the criminal "market", the strictly economic, perverse principles of which seem to paralyze all humanistic thoughts and actions towards the victims of social exclusion in our Western civilization.

As such, the overly prison-based approach has significant penological shortcomings. Paradoxically, sentences served within the community (currently imposed for just over one in ten convictions) seem not only more proportionate, but also less costly (except for the electronic monitoring of offenders) and more effective in reducing the social marginalization of convicted offenders.

Today, the loss of confidence in the criminal justice system is patently obvious. It is compounded by a misperception of criminal insecurity which, unlike the other forms of insecurity that plague some of our poorest citizens, is demonized politically and in the media and is wrongly equated with the fear of crime arising from the experience of victimization. So much so that victims, grouped with increasing frequency into associations to defend their a priori legitimate interests, have become heavily involved in the penal scene, and all the more so for the fact that they were long excluded from it.

At the same time, thanks to the obligations of a fair trial, victims are once again offered the place that they should never have lost, in their capacity as stakeholder alongside the offender and the state prosecutor. There can be no judicial truth (which is necessarily a joint construction) without that of the victim. Equality of arms is a democratic necessity, a requirement consistent with human rights and the fundamental principles of criminal law. Such a position is not self-evident, and there is much criticism regarding the current upsurge in "victimhood", allegedly the source of the increased severity of the social and correctional response towards offenders. Based, it seems, on the typically French rhetoric of denunciation, intellectualized views on the "fantasy", "classic", and "rival" victim do not stand up to a concrete analysis of the "ordinary"

---

[11]. A. Kensey, *Prison et récidive. Des peines de plus en plus longues : la société est-elle vraiment mieux protégée ?*, A. Colin, Coll. Sociétales, 2007, 79-159.

[12]. S. Portelli, *Récidivistes. Chroniques de l'humanité ordinaire*, Grasset, 2008; Kensey, Prison et récidive, 161-219; A. Benaouda, A. Kensey, La récidive des condamnés à la perpétuité, in *Cahiers d'études pénitentiaires et criminologiques*, 2008-24, multigraph., pub. Administration pénitentiaire.

[13]. On the demography of criminal activity, see Cario, Introduction aux sciences criminelles, p. 39ets. P.V. Tournier, *Dictionnaire de démographie pénale. Des outils pour arpenter le champ pénal*, L'Harmattan, Coll. Criminologie, 2010.

[14]. M. Chauvière et al., *L'indigent et le délinquant. Pénalisation de la pauvreté et privatisation de l'action sociale*, Fondation Copernic, 2008; L. Mucchielli, *L'invention de la violence. Des peurs, des chiffres, des faits*, Fayard, 2011.

victim's everyday legal experience.[15] Victims of serious offenses, who are taken into account throughout the penal process, particularly by Victim Services, contradict such intellectual flimsiness. This construction of victimhood—based on supposed social representations that are yet to be scientifically proven—in response to the law and order approach, without epistemic reflection, is similar in its excesses to the most populist penal claims.

In this context, restorative justice processes are likely to bring the work of justice closer to fulfillment. Drawing from traditional practices, such measures offer the supreme advantage of focusing both on punishing offenses and on repairing the harm done to people, with a view to restoring the social peace that is seriously compromised by crime. Based on the philosophical precept of "reintegrative shaming",[16] in this regard restorative justice intends to highlight the inacceptable nature of the offense committed and, consubstantially, to assert the love that friends, family, and the community continue to feel for the person who sincerely shoulders responsibility for the crime. Of course, it may only be applied to infringements of essential social values (felonies), as the treatment of antisocial behavior, breaches of social discipline, instances of deviance such as maladjustment (now unfairly penalized) do not belong to the field of criminal justice.

2. The conceptual aspects of restorative justice

There are several definitions of restorative justice available, illustrating the creativity encouraged by this alternative way of ensuring justice.[17] In concrete terms, it can be characterized by several key criteria which in turn validate as restorative the measures it promotes. Part of a dynamic process, restorative justice presupposes the voluntary participation of all those who feel concerned by the criminal conflict, in the presence and under the supervision of a "judicial third party" and, if necessary, of a "psychological and/or social third party". It requires the active involvement of each party in negotiations to find the best solutions for all concerned which, through their increased sense of responsibility, are likely to lead to restitution for all, and more broadly, to the restoration of social harmony.

The operationalization of restorative justice measures causes a real epistemic shift, to the undoubted benefit of the criminal justice system and in a fully complementary manner. In the current model of criminal justice, crime is considered as an act prejudicial to the State. The justice system focuses exclusively on the abstract responsibility of the offender and on the offense committed, with the aim of applying the penalty provided for by the law. Justice is viewed through an adversarial legal process with offenders and victims remaining passive or even ignored. As such, positive law reduces "criminal procedure to a technical matter".[18] The penalty provided by law is seen as fair in itself, and compliance outweighs results.

According to the restorative philosophy, crime is an offense causing harm to people and relationships. Consequently, the aim of the justice system is to identify the needs and obligations of each protagonist. Justice is understood as a process that actively involves all individuals concerned. Dialog is used to foster reciprocity and the sharing of emotions. Each stakeholder is encouraged to take practical responsibility, leading to a

---

[15]. See Cario, *Qui a peur des victimes?*, in *AJPénal*, Dalloz, 2004-12, 434-436; *AJPénal*, 2009-12, 491-494.

[16]. J. Braithwaite, *Crime, Shame and Reintegration* (1989) (Cambridge University Press, 1999).

[17] T. De Villette, *Faire justice autrement. Le défi des rencontres entre détenus et victimes*, Médiaspaul, 2009; Cario, *La justice restaurative*, 74 et seq.

[18] A. Garapon, D. Salas, *Les nouvelles sorcières de Salem. Leçons d'Outreau*, Seuil, 2007, 138.

search for consensual, forward-looking solutions intended to repair all harm. Here, both results and the process are essential, as the various measures available indicate.

Such a shift is beneficial to all stakeholders, due to the complementarity between the judge's consideration of the crime and of its perpetrator, and the consideration of the repercussions of a serious crime on social ties by the facilitators of restorative justice (professional or volunteer workers with appropriate training: mediators, negotiators, facilitators). All stakeholders—offenders, victims, and their families alike—have rights consistent with human rights and the fundamental principles of criminal law, which are applicable first and foremost from an ethical viewpoint. Recognition is a fundamental ethical position. According to Axel Honneth, relationships of social recognition are structured around three characteristics associated with love (a condition of self-confidence), rights (a condition of self-respect), and social solidarity (a condition of self-esteem).[19] Recognition is therefore "based on the experience of intersubjectivity [which implies] that the relationship is considered more important than the individual".[20] It is through the eyes of others that humanity is fulfilled, and that the humanity of the victim-as-subject and the offender-as-subject is founded. Or, as Gaston Bachelard puts it, "The I awakens by the grace of the Thou".[21] Consequently, the social relationship harmed by the crime can be restored when reciprocal recognition gives the individuals concerned the possibility to be reborn together.

Along with recognition, another vital component of the restorative process is the support and guidance given to the interested parties. Providing support means accompanying the person in the direction he or she is going, at his or her own speed. It also means empathetically sharing the suffering of the victim and, if need be, of the offender. This right to support implies that both be heard by professionals well versed in listening and interviewing techniques, at a pace that limits physical and psychological fatigue. The authenticity of their statements must be accepted, in accordance with the presumption of innocence and the presumption of victimity. They must also be understood, through the use of an interpreter where necessary.

Restoration must be comprehensive, complete, and effective, on both sides of the crime. To make amends is to take care of the other person as a victimized individual, with full respect for the complex nature of the suffering he or she has undergone. The reintegration of the victim or of his or her family into society is an essential duty. Having access to and support from skilled professionals is a fundamental right. It is only by respecting all of these conditions that each aspect of the victim's rights, and of the offender's rights, will be fulfilled at restoration.

It also appears an ethical necessity to punish the offender. When serious harm has been done to an essential social value and to the Common Good, naming the act, its perpetrator, and the victim is vital. Provided, that is, that the aforementioned rights to recognition, support, and reparation are respected. This includes for any victimization previously suffered by the offender, which cannot be dissociated from the crime for which he or she is being punished, with a view to his or her future social reintegration—the "official" idea behind the modern criminal justice system.

---

[19] A. Honneth, *The Struggle for Recognition: The Moral Grammar of Social Conflicts* (Polity Press, 1996) [*La lutte pour la reconnaissance*, Le Cerf, 1992/2010, 116etseq].

[20] H. Guéguen, G. Malochet, *Les théories de la reconnaissance*, La Découverte, Coll. Repères, 2012, 53-54.

[21] Préface, In M. Buber, *Je et tu* (1935), Aubier Montaigne, Coll. Bibliothèque philosophique, 1992, 8-9, [translated from French, "Le moi s'éveille par la grâce du toi"].

When legal proceedings are initiated, which obviously occurs in the case of serious crime (except when there are serious grounds for not doing so, such as the death of the offender or mental incapacitation), the rights of individuals must be consistent with the fundamental principles guaranteed by human rights and criminal procedure. Equality of arms is essential if the work of justice is to lead to a manifestation of truth, the punishment of the offender, the reparation of the victim, and the reestablishment of social peace. Today, these goals are rarely achieved at once. The reductionist strategy developed more or less consciously by our criminal justice system may nevertheless be significantly rectified by introducing measures of restorative justice in a genuinely complementary manner.

3. Implementation of restorative justice processes

Processes of restorative justice are diverse in origin and nature, but all have in common the desire to promote an encounter between offender and victim, and sometimes even their relatives. They are designed to play a part in all stages of the criminal procedure, usually "face to face": as an alternative to prosecution (in the case of lesser offenses that would benefit from being decriminalized), during the investigation and the trial, and post-sentencing, or even at the end of the sentence. The most serious offenses should not be excluded a priori; quite the opposite, provided that the conditions outlined above in the definition are met.

Victim–offender mediation[22] gives the interested parties the opportunity for a voluntary meeting to discuss the characteristics, consequences, and repercussions of the criminal conflict which opposes them. This restorative justice measure, also known as the Kitchener experiment, first emerged in Ontario, Canada in the early 1970s. *Victim Offender Reconciliation Programs* (*VORP*) soon became widespread in the United States, and then throughout Europe under the name *Victim Offender mediation* (*VOM*). Criminal mediation (reserved for adults) and criminal restitution involving minors are directly derived from these programs (see 4 January 1993, art. 41-1 of the Criminal Code and 12-1 Ord. 1945).

Family group conferences[23], inspired by the customs of the "Whanau" (extended family) of New Zealand's native Maori, whose extended family ties are very strong, are intended to deal with offenses committed by minors. Reintroduced in the 1980s, in 1989 they were incorporated into New Zealand's criminal legislation to be proposed systematically before initiation of any criminal proceedings against minors. Today, *Family Group Conferences* (*FGCs*) are implemented in Australia, the United States, Canada, the United Kingdom, and Belgium. Restorative conferences generally pursue the same objectives as victim/offender mediation, but see the offender, the victim, and the mediator/facilitator joined by a diverse group of participants. Any person or institution with an interest in the conflict being resolved and/or who may provide some form of support to the main stakeholders is welcome to be involved. The conference provides an opportunity to consider the means of support that the family or social environment is able to give the interested parties to help them recover their place in the community.

---

[22] M.S. Umbreit et al., *The Handbook of Victim Offender Mediation: An Essential Guide to Practice and Research* (Jossey-Bass Inc., 2001).

[23] A. MacRae, H. Zehr, *The Little Book of Family Group Conferences. New Zealand Style: A Hopeful Approach when Youth Cause Harm* (Good Books Pub., 2004); B. Sayous, Les conférences du groupe familial, in *La Justice restaurative. Une utopie qui marche?*, eds R. Cario and P. Mbanzoulou, L'Harmattan, Coll. Controverses, 2011, 33-48.

Circle sentencing[24] is a modern adaptation of indigenous practices of the First Nations of North America. Symbolizing equality, inclusiveness, the earth, and the life cycle, this practice seeks to appease the conflictual parties (victim, offender, their families and friends, and most importantly the community) in the presence of elders, under the supervision and with the support, depending on the custom, of their lawyers and representatives of legal institutions. Circle sentencing was integrated into the contemporary criminal justice system in the 1980s in order to strengthen links between cultures and to share the administration of justice.

Other, similar measures exist, including Truth and Reconciliation Commissions (TRC)[25] and Circles of Support and Accountability (CoSA).[26] Victim–offender encounters are distinctive in that they offer, after conviction, a dialog between a "group" of anonymous victims and prisoners.[27]

Each of these restorative justice initiatives takes place according to a fairly similar protocol, with two main preconditions: the whole process must be controlled by an experienced professional, and it must be the object of extremely careful preparation. Four phases are generally identified—eligibility (of the case and of the people involved), the encounter, the negotiations, and the monitoring of the agreement—with sometimes significant variations, depending particularly on whether the process adopted is pre- or post-sentence.[28]

They lead to various agreements concerning the repercussions of the crime, over and above its direct consequences (punishment of the offense, compensation for the various types of damages) that come under the sole responsibility of the judge. Firstly, during the exchanges facilitated as part of process, it may be a case of addressing the reasons for which the crime was committed against a given person, under given circumstances. Questions of "why" and "how" are not only essential for victims and their families, but also in a way for offenders' families and for the offenders themselves (in terms of taking into account the concrete reality of victimizations resulting in their offense). The next step may involve negotiating the best solutions for restoring, in highly practical terms, the various aspects of everyday life both within the family and socially. The fact that, in the vast majority of cases, serious crimes occur between people who know each other (through the family or workplace) makes this all the more important. The offenders' sincerity helps victims to assimilate apologies in various forms, thereby encouraging offenders to take responsibility. The commitments made by the communities present during the process inevitably increase its chance of success.

4. Evaluation of restorative practices

---

[24] M. Jaccoud, Les cercles de guérison et les cercles de sentence autochtones au Canada, *Criminologie*, 1999-32-1, 79-105; J., Dickson-Gilmore, C. La Prairie, *Will the Circle be Unbroken? Aboriginal Communities, Restorative Justice and the challenges of conflict and change* (University of Toronto Press, 2005).

[25] S. Leman-Langlois, *Réconciliation et justice* (Athéna, 2008).

[26] J.J. Goulet, "Et si c'était ma fille?," in *La Justice restaurative*, eds. R. Cario, P. Mbanzoulou, 63-68.

[27] See Infra, chapter by P. Mbanzoulou; R. Cario (eds.), *Les rencontres détenus-victimes. L'humanité retrouvée* (L'Harmattan, Coll. Controverses, 2012).

[28] R. Cario, *La justice restaurative*, 122etseq.

The satisfaction of those having participated in one of the above restorative processes is very real. Assessed scientifically, the feelings of stakeholders—such as having obtained justice, and of feeling a physical, psychological, and even psychosomatic relief—converge. The recognition offered by the restorative process is emphasized by all as the condition for possible closure (or its consolidation) among other human beings, since having the chance to give one's own point of view helps repair harm, regardless of the seriousness of the crime.[29] Magistrates and social and legal professionals consider measures of restorative justice to be perfectly complementary with the criminal justice system, a means to humanize the process and save time for all involved.[30] Socialized in this manner, the desire for "vindictive and destructive vengeance" fades to make way for sharing, reciprocity, mutual understanding, and vindication, which restores participants to a proactive state and allows them to regain power over their lives. The fear of crime derived from experience fades through listening to the offenders, to the sincerity of their regrets and to their commitments for the future.

As well as savings in legal, health, and social services costs, it should also be noted—and this is not the least important—that offenders' increased sense of accountability results in a much lower rate of recidivism. The process helps offenders realize that they belong to the community, and that it is willing to take them back after they have paid their dues. They can thus clearly gauge that it is the act they committed which is stigmatized as unacceptable, whereas they themselves are still people, and have a rightful place among other human beings.

To conclude, provisionally, restorative justice unquestionably holds great promise. There is nothing surprising in that. Whereas traditional criminal justice responds to the *consequences* of crime (punishment of offenders in view of their social rehabilitation, payment of damages to the victim), in favor of the direct protagonists, and more rarely to the benefit of the families on either the giving or the receiving ends of crime, it fails to address the *repercussions* of crime, which are many, deep, and painful. In processes of restorative justice, everything that affected the daily life of those touched by the crime (victim, offender, family and friends, community, neighbors) is considered. Responses are negotiated between all parties to best meet the needs of some, the obligations of others, and the possibilities of all,[31] under the supervision and with the validation of the "judicial third party" and the "psychological or social third party".

Therefore, it is urgent for restorative justice to be incorporated into the French criminal justice landscape. Apart from criminal mediation (for adults only, and only during prosecution) and criminal restitution for minors (fortunately more likely to be ruled at all stages of the procedure), the French restorative arsenal is sorely lacking. Especially since the existing measures are intended more to "take a bite out" of dismissals rather than the prosecutions themselves (including with regard to minors, as 90% of measures are ruled by the public prosecutor's department), and therefore resemble

---

[29] I. Aertsen, "Victim-offender mediation with serious offenses," in *Crime Policy in Europe. Good Practices and Promising Sample*, ed. Conseil de l'Europe, 2005, 75-86.

[30] L.W. Sherman, H. Strang (eds.), *Restorative Justice: The Evidence* (Smith Institute pub., 2007), smith-institute.org.uk; R. Cario, *La justice restaurative*, 138 et seq. and ref. cited; J. Shapland, G. Robinson, A. Sorsby, *Restorative Justice in Practice: Evaluating What Works for Victims and Offenders* (Willan Publishing, 2010).

[31] On these points, see R. Cario, *Victimologie. De l'effraction du lien intersubjectif à la restauration sociale,* L'Harmattan, Coll. Traité de sciences criminelles, Vol. 2-1, Third Edition. 2006, 144 et seq.

punitive additions likely to expand, excessively, the scope of penal sanctions set by the contemporary bodies of social control.[32] Nonetheless, optimism of action must not yield to the pessimism of the intellect. The Offender–Victim Encounter series set up in the Poissy central penitentiary in 2010 augurs remarkable prospects if the legislature chooses to give it the force of law.[33] In the same vein, a few restorative-leaning penalties, by fully involving the victim, could well contribute to the fulfillment of justice.[34] Through the complementarity between the criminal justice system (which deals with the consequences of the offense) and restorative justice (which deals with its repercussions), the issue of the victim's existence itself is no longer taboo, because the measures it advocates are concerned with everyone, the offender as much as relatives and members of their communities. This is a key point, because scientific and clinical victimology now highlights the extreme vulnerability of the protagonists, their close relationship, and the interchangeability of their roles throughout their personal history and their social background. The prevention of and fight against criminal activity, on both sides of crime, is a socially complex issue. To understand and tackle it necessarily requires a transdisciplinary approach, which will be ensured, finally, by the integration of criminology into University programs.[35]

Let us not forget too easily, however, that victims could become a thing of the past if prevention (particularly early prevention) were reinstated as the sole purpose of public policies for harmonious, inclusive social integration, a source of personal fulfillment and the best defense from the aggressive (auto- and hetero-) resolution of the intersubjective strife that floods our society. This is simply a rational utopianism, in the Bourdieusian sense, which plays on the knowledge of what is probable in order to achieve the possible.

---

[32] On these ideas, see. S. Cohen, The punitive city: note on the dispersal of the social control, in *Contemporary crisis*, 1979-3, 339-363; Cario, *La justice restaurative*, 142 et seq.

[33] Cario, Mbanzoulou, Les rencontres détenus victimes à la Maison centrale de Poissy: un retour d'expérience, in *Les chroniques du CIRAP*, 2011-11 (Pub. Ecole Nationale d'Administration Pénitentiaire); R. Cario (ed.), *Les RDV*, L'Harmattan, Coll. Controverses, forthcoming, 2012.

[34] Cario, *La justice restaurative*, 163etseq.; T. Clay, P. Joxe, C. Lazerges, J.P. Mignnard (eds.), *Manifeste pour la Justice*, Le cherche midi, Coll. Documents, 2012, 15.

[35] R. Cario, M. Herzog-Evans, L.M. Villerbu, *La criminologie à l'Université. Mythes… et réalités*, L'Harmattan, Coll. Controverses, 2012.

Further reading

Aertsen, I. et al. 2004. *Renouer les liens sociaux. Médiation et justice réparatrice en Europe*, Strasbourg: Pub. Conseil de l'Europe.

Barats, T., B. Fellegi, and S.Windt, eds. 2012. *Responsibility-taking, Relationship-building and Restoration in Prisons*. Budapest: P-T Mühely publisher.

Elliott, E., and R.M. Gordon. 2005. *New Directions in Restorative Justice. Issues, Practice, Evaluation*, Vancouver: Willan Publishing.

Gailly, P., 2011. *La justice restauratrice. Textes réunis et traduits par....* Bruxelles: Larcier, Coll. Crimen.

Hinton, A.L., ed. 2011. *Transitional Justice. Global Mechanisms and Local Realities after Genocide and Mass Violence*. Rutgers University Press.

Johnstone, G., and D. Van Ness, eds. 2007. *Handbook of Restorative Justice*. Cullompton: Willan Publishing, 650.

Senon, J.L., G. Lopez, and R. Cario (Dir.), 2012. *Psychocriminologie. Prévention, prise en charge, expertise*. Second Edition, Paris: Dunod.

Ventura Miller, H., ed. *Restorative Justice: From Theory to Practice, Sociology of Crime, Law and Deviance*, 2008-11, JAI Press Inc.

Zehr, H., and B. Toews, eds. 2004. *Critical Issues in Restorative Justice*. New York: Criminal Justice Press and Monsey: Willan Publishing .

Zehr, H. 2012. *La justice restaurative. Pour sortir des impasses de la logique punitive*. Genève: Labor et Fides.

About the Author

Robert Cario serves as Professor of Criminology, Director of the Jean Pinatel Unit for Comparative Criminology, and Joint Director of the Master of Criminology at the Université de Pau et des Pays de l'Adour (UJP/CRAJ)

Subprime or subcrime? The criminal dimension of the financial crises: an astonishing denial of reality

Jean-François Gayraud

Subprime loans were the cause of the greatest financial and subsequently economic crisis since 1929. In the United States, for example, the social impact was immense with millions of households suffering repossessions, mass unemployment, the disappearance of savings invested in the stock market, and a jump in the poverty rate from 12.5% to 14.3% between 2007 and 2009.

Anesthetic explanations

It is therefore vital to consider the true origins of this tragedy: fundamentally, what does the term "subprime crisis" mean? All are keen to impose a happy narrative on the causes of the crisis through explanations which are either fatalistic (cycle theory), magical (a catastrophe, a cataclysm), or mollifying (market failures). Not to mention the reassuring reflections of Doctor Panglosses who claim that *"this crisis is a roughly psychological one"* (Alain Minc). These denial specialists are often those who were blind to the growing anomie in financial markets during the boom years (1980/2000). Having failed to anticipate the crisis (if they did not cause it), they have since been falling over themselves to conceal their deepest doubts, thus spelling the nearly universal collapse of academic and media expertise on both sides of the Atlantic.

However, there is another possible diagnosis that reveals the true nature of Wall Street and a new balance of power in the United States, and more broadly the increasing autonomy of players on the globalized financial market. In order to understand the hidden roots of this crisis, we need to think outside the box imposed by propriety. The subprime crisis was a systemic fraud.[1] More than just a metaphor, a criminological approach reveals the existence of a series of genuine frauds which, rather than simply being accidents, were in fact symptoms of a system that had become anomic. Ultimately, American finance has become a vast crime scene. Few financial crises have had such a clear criminal dimension or critical mass of frauds.[2] As always, published opinion—belonging to the elite with access to the media—is in a hurry to demonize any such troubling viewpoints by resorting to easy fear-mongering: Conspiracy theories, scapegoats, distractions, populism. Using crime to explain a macroeconomic phenomenon may seem derisory, anecdotal, even naïve. However, it is vital for anyone wishing to explore the roots of a crisis caused by human actions alone. A criminological reading can pull back the thick veil concealing institutional, extremely lucrative tartuffery. A crime-based approach also has the advantage of bringing the economy back

---

1. For details of this thesis, with accompanying bibliography, please refer to our book: Jean-François Gayraud, *La grande fraude: Crime, subprimes et crises financiers* (Odile Jacob, 2011). Also: Jean-François Gayraud, "Subprimes: Crise innommable, donc incurable. Ou comment récompenser les fraudeurs," in *La finance pousse-au-crime*, ed. Xavier Raufer (Choiseul, 2011).
2. On the history of financial crises and their fraudulent dimension: Charles K. Kindleberger and Robert Aliber. *Manias, Panics, and Crashes: A History of Financial Crisis* (John Wiley & Sons, 2005). On the role of fraud in periods of boom: Robert J. Shiller, *Irrational Exuberance* (Doubleday, 2005).

to the real world and its "animal instincts" (J.M. Keynes),3 far from the abstractions and abuses of mathematical modeling.4

Despite today's constant references to the Great Depression, no-one seems to remember the United States Congress's "Pecora Commission"5 whose hearings (1932–1934) revealed massive financial malpractice by establishment "robber barons" to an indignant public. President Franklin D. Roosevelt made skilful use of this widespread indignation to push through his major reform laws. The lesson of the senate hearings and the reforms enacted is clear: unregulated markets will inevitably descend into speculative and fraudulent excesses.

Dogmatic and criminogenic market deregulation

From the 1980s onwards, oversight and blindness began to take over.6 America, followed by parts of the rest of the world, began a dogmatic deregulation of its markets with criminogenic consequences. Criminogenic in the strict meaning of the term: new opportunities and impetuses for fraud were made available to the least scrupulous economic and financial players. For the subprime crisis has a history—it was not an accident, nor an isolated event. In fact, it is simply the most recent in a long list of criminal failures and crises spreading across a generation: the collapse of savings and loan associations,7 then of numerous multinational companies including the giant Enron, representing the epitome of the "rogue stage of financialized capitalism". However, when the financial and real estate bubble linked to subprime lending burst, the standard explanations immediately returned (economic cycles, greed, etc.). Economists attempted to use well-oiled but short-sighted concepts (market asymmetry, moral hazard, defaulting loans, etc.) to explain circumstances which they had previously failed to foresee. This was done with a certain level of discomfort, however, as economic science not only failed to predict the subprime crisis but also partly helped to trigger it by promoting an unreal vision of supposedly efficient and self-regulating (and thus infallible) markets.8 This crisis can be traced back to clear ideological roots. However, the "invisible hand of the market" is only a representation; moreover a quasi-religious one, with questionable scientific merit; by contrast, the "invisible hand of crime" working on unmonitored markets is always proven. Deregulation born of public policies thus initiated a cycle of criminal finance punctuated by fraudulent financial crises and collapses.

---

3. George A. Akerlof and Robert J. Shiller. *Animal Spirits: How Human Psychology Drives the Economy, and Why it Matters for Global Capitalism* (Princeton University Press, 2009).
4. Excessive modeling has clearly resulted in excessive simplification and specialization. This is known as scientism.
5. Michael Perino. *The Hellhound of Wall Street: How Ferdinand Pecora's Investigation of the Great Crash Forever Changed American Finance* (Penguin Books, 2010).
6. On this concept of blindness:Xavier Raufer. *Les nouveaux dangers planétaires*. Coll. Biblis. CNRS éditions, 2012. Also:Jean-François Gayraud and François Thual. *Géostratégie du crime* (Odile Jacob, 2012).
7. Gayraud. *La grande fraude*. Also general literature on the subject: William K. Black, *The Best Way to Rob a Bank is to Own One* (University of Texas Press, 2005).
8. The ultra-liberal doxa has successfully attached itself to the edges of science, and thus gained an important legitimacy, thanks to multiple Nobel prizes during the 1970s and 1990s. On this ideology and its role in the economic and financial history of the United States: John Cassidy. *How Markets Fail: The Logic of Economic Calamities*. Farrar, Straus and Giroux, 2010. Also:James K. Galbraith, *The Predator State: How Conservatives Abandoned the Free Market and Why Liberals Should Too* (*L'Etat prédateur: Comment la droite a renoncé au marché libre et pourquoi la gauche devrait en faire autant*. Seuil, 2009).

From traditional fraud to innovative fraud

In order to understand some of the hidden roots of this crisis, we need to think outside the box of the common patterns prescribed by the mediasphere. So what do we find? Series of genuine (systematic) frauds have polluted every single real estate and financial market (the system), helping to create speculative bubbles. Something out of the ordinary emerges: "Crime scenes" on a macroeconomic scale which enable this to be reclassified as a "subcrime" crisis. The long and opaque financial chain of subprime loans evolved into a "food chain" attracting multiple predators, with almost no obstacles in their way thanks to deregulation. There are two possible approaches to describing this systemic criminal predation.

An initial analytical approach on both a macrocriminological and a macroeconomic level demonstrates how the entire American financial system was reorganized following the collapse of savings and loan associations to prompt a massive transfer of wealth from the poorest to the richest in American society, at a time when a lack of desire to distribute purchasing power to those on the lowest incomes (income and salary stagnation) meant that they were sold an illusion of enrichment through an ill-considered and cynical development of debt. Deregulation was a concomitant of greater inequality at a level not seen since the nineteenth century, temporarily hidden by those in power by encouraging debt, off-balance-sheet activities, and securitization. However, is it possible to handcuff cynical public policies, or dreams ("a house for all") which have transformed into nightmares?

A second approach, this time on a microcriminological and microeconomic level, seems even more relevant to our demonstration. The apparent complexity of the system thus barely conceals two major frauds. First of all, we discover a more traditional and unpolished fraud consisting of encouraging modest and vulnerable households (which are in theory not solvent or barely solvent) to take out loans which will inevitably choke them. The nicknames given to these loans perfectly sum up their true nature: they are known as "liar" or "predatory" loans. They explicitly target the weakest members of American society: ethnic minorities—in particular blacks and Hispanics—as well as the poor, the handicapped, and senior citizens. These fungible categories, for example poor and black senior citizens, are urged to take on more debt than they are able to repay, intentionally deceived by cynical professionals. Even worse, these loans are described as "neutron loans", which (like the eponymous bomb) kill the people and leave the houses. In fact, these subprime/liar/predatory loans are "ghost" loans—also known as NINJA loans as they intentionally target households with no income, no job, and no assets. These explicit qualifiers describing the true nature of these loans were not invented a posteriori by sensationalist commentators, but instead were used right from the outset by financial professionals themselves. The terms thus reveal their guilty intentions and consequently make a mockery of any attempts to claim ignorance or incompetence. All of these loans are concentrations of plainly criminal acts: breach of trust, fraud, abuse of weakness, forgery, etc.9

A posteriori evaluation of these subprime loans is overwhelming. At least three-quarters of all cases involved an element of deceit! Mortgage lenders and their lobbyists, the mortgage brokers, are in practice two professions with little regulation where monitoring and controls are slack. Mortgage lenders are also a central element of what is

---

9. For a more detailed description of the landscape, far from economic theory, and of the formation of this fraudulent real-estate bubble: Richard Bitner. *Confessions of a Subprime Lender: An Insider' Stale of Greed, Fraud, and Ignorance* (John Wiley & Sons, 2008).

known as "shadow banking". Therefore, in the absence of any real regulation, bad (dishonest) professionals gradually replaced the good (honest) ones and bad practices superseded good ones, like a new Gresham's law on a major scale.

Secondly, we now have an innovative and globalized fraud, modern in a manner of speaking, consisting of dispersing these questionable loans by removing them from the balance sheets of financial institutions. This time, the victims were not average Americans but international investors. The fraudulent real-estate bubble was followed by an equally large financial bubble. Subprime/predatory loans were transformed into financial securities: securitized. Mortgage lenders understood that securitizing high-risk loans left them as sure-fire winners. They ceded legal and financial responsibility for these loans with a high likelihood of default (due to their fraudulent nature), and also immediately cashed in the liquid assets. The securitization process thus encouraged them to pursue loan policies, which were not qualitative (prudential) but rather quantitative (always more), even as far as fraud. Risk taking was at a maximum, as the income earned by these professionals was index-linked to the volume of loans. The technique of securitization had been praised by dogmatic liberals and monetarists (such as Alan Greenspan) as a factor in spreading risk. Instead, it was an instrument infecting the entire financial chain. Questionable loans were regrouped—and in fact hidden—in debt packages (automobile loans, student loans, etc.), with the bad apples (subprime/predatory loans) contaminating the rest of the basket. With these "innovative new financial products" (CDOs etc.), the sorcerer's apprentices of Wall Street believed that they could suddenly turn lead (bad debts) into gold (sustainable profits). These alchemists of innovative finance imagined that they were defying the laws of financial gravity and common sense, blinded by euphoria and profits, making themselves believe that "this time it's different".10

These new financial products, toxic in nature due to being crippled by subprime loans, contaminated the entire American and subsequently global financial system, producing a chaotic butterfly effect: small fraudulent causes, large macroeconomic consequences. At this stage, deceit was being skillfully spearheaded by those responsible for ensuring *de facto* regulation of the financial markets: The three main rating agencies, one of which is French (Fitch),11 and the major investment banks (Goldman Sachs, Lehman Brothers, etc.).

The record of the rating agencies is a painful one.12 The 9/10 ratings given to securitized products would prove to be erroneous. Such incompetence is stunning. These massive errors can surely be explained by the fact that the loan files they received were booby-trapped with fudged figures by mortgage lenders, mortgage brokers, and sometimes even households themselves. However, ratings with this level of fantasy can also be traced back to the two "conflicts of interest" governing these agencies' economic model. First of all, the agencies are paid by the issuers of securities (issuer-pay principle),

---

10. Carmen M. Reinhart and Kenneth S. Rogoff. *Cette fois, c'est différent: Huit siècles de folie financière.* Pearson, 2010. The phrase "this time it's different" (*cette fois, c'est different*) is simply a manifestation of the blindness we have already touched upon.

11. The French press has always been very reticent regarding this rating agency's role in the crisis, most likely because it belongs to the FIMLAC group which is owned by French capitalism baron Marc Ladreit de Lacharrière.

12. Rating agencies are structurally short-sighted. They failed to anticipate the financial crises of Latin America in the 1980s, the collapse of the American savings and loan associations and the giant Enron, the Greek sovereign debt sinkhole, etc. In fact, they tend to give yesterday's forecast or announce catastrophes which are then triggered by their pronouncements (self-fulfilling prophecies).

a fact which does not encourage critical thinking and foresight, particularly with the ratings market becoming increasingly lucrative: who would bite the hand that feeds them so well? Secondly, agencies are involved in the upstream structuring of innovative financial products, in theory in different departments (the Chinese wall principle): Is it conceivable that a restaurant guide could offer impartial evaluations of restaurants it owned?

As for the large Wall Street investment banks, their fraudulent record is equally substantial. They tried to present themselves as the victims once the crisis emerged, forgetting that they were in fact working at the upstream end of the financial chain. These merchant banks were the financers and sometimes even the owners of dishonest mortgage lenders. Right from the outset, therefore, they were the financers and dealers of the highly addictive drug that subprime loans and "innovative financial products" became. Furthermore, the Wall Street merchant banks also directly indulged in multiple forms of malpractice. Massaging their accounts to hide losses linked to subprime loans, failing to advise investors on the level of risk associated with securitized products, betting that the securities offered to their clients would fall, manipulating the interbank lending rates (Libor, Eurobor), etc. Ultimately, bankers and rating agencies colluded to deceive purchasers/investors regarding the actual quality of "innovative financial products". Despite such a high level of malpractice which became so glaring after 2007/2008, fraudulent activities continued after the outbreak of the crisis, this time as part of "loan renegotiation/alteration" operations and foreclosures (foreclosure-gate).

White-collar organized crime

Let there be no doubt regarding the criminological species in question here. While "traditional gangsters" (organized crime) were able to benefit from the windfall, the architects and main beneficiaries of these frauds were primarily members of the respectable elite installed in high and select society. Moreover, was it not an American sociologist, Edwin H. Sutherland, who invented the concept of "white-collar crime" in the 1930s?[13] However, this concept seems to have been rather surpassed in the present day. In effect, on close examination the white-collar fraudsters of globalized finance reveal planning and association. We also ask ourselves why the organizational and managerial powers retained a monopoly of the traditional gangsters (organized crime)? What has been (newly) unveiled by the subprime crisis is the emergence of an unfamiliar "white-collar organized crime/criminality".[14]

However, the record of criminal convictions is disappointing, to the point of being pathetic. In the face of so much fraud, the American courts proved unable to react in credible fashion. They punished only the dishonest borrowers (speculating households, opportunistic gangsters) but no financial professionals—with the sole exception of one low-level banker. However, 80% of fraud is attributable to them. Why this impunity? First of all, the production of evidence is always a delicate operation for crimes which are invisible, complex, and committed by intelligent individuals embedded deep in a system which they helped to create. Secondly, in accordance with a stubborn tradition, the justice system and federal regulation agencies often prefer to "wipe the slate clean" with agreements negotiated on a penal or civil level (plea bargaining, settlement). The rating agencies escaped the long arm of the law by taking refuge behind the First Amendment to

---

13. Edwin H. Sutherland. *White Collar Crime: The Uncut Version* (Yale University Press, 1983). Also, an earlier book on the criminality of the elite written in 1907 by an American sociologist: Edward Alsworth Ross. *Sin and Society: An Analysis of Latter-day Iniquity* (Bibliolife, 1907).
14. We suggested this new approach in Gayraud, *La grande fraude*.

the United States Constitution guaranteeing freedom of expression. The agencies were granted the status of press agencies, rather than financial institutions: offering opinions rather than providing ratings.

As has become clear, the American federal system never wanted credible means to deal with waves of white-collar crime on a macroeconomic level. Admittedly, the diversion effect produced by the "war on terrorism" prevented the American police and justice system from focusing on the criminals of the upperworld. The American police and justice system found themselves swamped by a wave of crimes, too numerous and too opaque, while their manpower was dedicated to tracking down Al-Qaeda as the hypothetical priority.

The tragicomedy that has been played out on Wall Street for the past 30 years remains the same: Rogue bankers (banksters) pay lip service to confessing their sins, pay a fine, promise not to do it again, then reoffend a few years later. What conclusion can be drawn from this? That impunity serves to encourage repeated offences, both for bank robbers and a for rogue bankers/financiers. In accordance with the doctrine of "too big to fail" (financial systems) which has prompted the American federal authorities to save questionable and interconnected financial institutions, the failure to punish thus highlights the new reality of "too big to prosecute, too big to jail" (financial fraud): Too big to prosecute/jail, and consequently both intimidating and extortionate.

Frauds on financial markets are a matter of breathtaking routine, accidentally revealed in isolated incidents of rare legal cases or systemic crises. It is a kind of normalization of deviance and crime. This crisis comes from "on high", just like those which were once so commonplace in the Third World and were viewed with such condescension by the West. Published in 2011, the United States Congress's two voluminous reports on the financial crisis (hearings held by the Financial Crisis inquiry Commission, or FCIC15; and work undertaken by Senator Carl Levin) returned a bleak picture of Wall Street and left no doubt regarding the criminal dimension of this crisis. Frauds appear to be the common thread explaining the origin of the subprime crisis.

"Madoffified" finance, a trapped system...

The massive fraud (60 billion dollars?) perpetrated by Bernard Madoff—incidentally revealed as a result of the subprime crisis, like collateral damage—was not an aberration but rather the symptom of an American finance and economy system in general that had become pyramid-shaped, as if "Madoffified". Bernard Madoff simply performed on his own personal (microeconomic) scale what America had allowed to happen on a large (macroeconomic) scale for a generation: a pyramid of private debts reeking of fraud. The same context of blind deregulation incentivizing fraud produced both the subprime crisis and the Madoff affair; moreover, numerous other fraudulent pyramids subsequently emerged when the guardians of the temple (financial market authorities, etc.) finally awoke.

The real question behind this crisis, however, is a political rather than strictly legal one. Where do such destructive and criminal laws of deregulation come from? Since the 1980s, the powerful Wall Street finance lobby has been able to literally and legally trap—in fact purchase—a large part of the American political class, followed by Washington's institutions.16 The now astronomical costs of electoral campaigns mean that the

---

15. *The Financial Crisis Inquiry Report: Final Report of the National Commission on the Causes of the Financial and Economic Crisis in the United States* (Public Affairs, 2011).
16. Galbraith, *The Predator State*, Op. cit. Also: Simon Johnson and James Kwak. *13 Bankers: The Wall Street takeover and the Next Financial Meltdown* (Pantheon Books, 2010).

American political system puts elected representatives with more money at a significant advantage. Concerned about its privileges, the powerful finance lobby only supports Democrat and Republican candidates who have been won over to their deregulation cause. These laws are thus sold to a financial oligarchy. We therefore see a transfer of power from Wall Street to Washington—and this geopolitical swing is facilitated by the questionable practice of "revolving doors" between the financial industry and the upper echelons of federal administration. This practice creates infinite "conflicts of interests" conducive to real instances of corruption, or at the very least to an osmosis of interests and points of view between financiers and political/administrative decision makers. This broadly criminal crisis brings up to date the new balance of powers in the United States between politics (Washington) and finance (Wall Street); is the "military-industrial complex" denounced by President Eisenhower (1961) being followed by a surreptitiously imposed "political-financial complex"?[17] Moreover, this is most likely a new balance of power common to numerous countries across the world. The finance lobby is not content to limit itself to part of the American political class. It has successfully attached itself to academics,[18] financial analysts, and finally journalists trapped by the complexity of the subject matter and the majority of media's membership of major capitalist groups. Fraud has thus managed to disappear from mainstream analysis. Is that not precisely the perfect crime—one where reality is ignored, or better still where the idea itself seems inconceivable?

A predatory system remains intact

The predatory system behind this social disaster has remained intact, even following the Dodd-Frank financial regulation law passed in the summer of 2010. Despite its bulk, this law has proven to be a paper tiger whose rare binding standards for American finance were steamrolled by the finance lobby during the legislation editing process. It is a far cry from the New Deal laws which successfully stood up to the financial powers.

Ironically, or in a barely concealed logic of the system, the institutions and individuals most responsible for this criminal disaster have themselves emerged from the crisis stronger than ever. What, then, should we think of a system which ultimately rewards the fraudsters so well? This is a troubling status quo, since this criminal diagnosis was made by Americans themselves through Congress's Inquiry Commissions. This was clearly insufficient, suggesting that the "power of the word" (executive, legislative, and media power) no longer carries any weight in the face of the "power of the real" (money). Like the genie of the lamp, the players in globalized finance have broken free with no-one now able or willing to discipline them.

---

17. In 1956 American sociologist Charles Wright published *The power elite* which describes the new American ruling elite, whose main characteristic is their capacity to circulate between three echelons of power: The economy, politics, and the military. He denounces an immoral and concentrated elite able to rely on "celebrities", the product of mass media, and on "intellectual tightrope walkers". Nothing has really changed since then—at most, the addition of finance to the triangle of power.

18. On the complicity of certain academics, well paid by the financial industry, and the conflicts of interest affecting them, the 2010 documentary *Inside jobs* written, produced, and directed by Charles H. Ferguson is currently the best reference. The real issue is in fact to establish cause and consequence. Are they chosen because they profess "good" ideas a priori, or do they accommodate them a posteriori because they have agreed to endorse positions which are favorable to the financial industry?

About the Author

Jean-François Gayraud is a Doctor in Law, graduate of the Paris Institute of Political Studies (IEP) and of the Paris Institute of Criminology. A former student of the French national police academy (ENSP), he is a Police Superintendent.

His published works include *"Le monde des mafias. Géopolitique du crime organisé"* (Odile Jacob, 2005), *"La grande fraude. Crime, subprimes et crises financières"* (Odile Jacob, 2011), *"Le renseignement criminel"* with François Farcy (CNRS éditions, 2011), and *"Géostratégie du crime"* with François Thual (Odile Jacob, 2012). He has also published an article entitled "Geostrategy of Criminality. Highly Intensive Criminality," in *The McGraw-Hill Homeland Security Handbook*, ed. David Kamien, 2012.

International Journal on Criminology—Volume 1—Number 1—Fall 2013

Demographic Analysis of the Penal System: A Different Approach to Sentencing

Pierre V. Tournier

At the end of the 1970s, with an education in the physical sciences, mathematics, and demography, I became unexpectedly involved in the study of a rather unusual population—the prison population. The French National Correctional Administration was in the process of computerizing its systems and was seeking to analyze the statistical data that would emerge from these new systems. It was somewhat by chance that they recruited a demographer, rather than a statistician, for this task.

Since then and for nearly 35 years, I have worked in the criminological field and sought, through quantitative analysis, to shed new light on *prison trends and issues*. My research on prison demography has focused both on "populations under correctional control" (whether detained or monitored in the community) and on the administrative and judicial decision processes that impact these populations. This work has encouraged me to reflect on the terms and concepts employed by those who have initiated criminal justice and prison policies, that is, those who hold a direct or indirect stake in these policies (i.e., judges, prison staff, unions and professional or associated organizations, the media, etc.). These policies have targeted issues such as clearance rates, the growth or reduction of the prison population, prison overcrowding, alternative sanctions, the enforcement of criminal sanctions, early release decisions, as well as the rates of recidivism or returns to prison and the prevalence of repeat offenders. These political terms commonly used in the penal system needed to be revisited with the rigor required of any serious quantitative approach. The goal was to better understand the changes in the penal field and make comparisons within the European context, and to create explanatory and evaluative tools regarding promising policies.

I thus sought to formalize the results of this long-term work, and to analyze everyday vocabulary and its evolution over time. My aim was to define these concepts, as well as to create new concepts, and to include them within the public discourse in France and in other countries. The materials required for such a study was first gathered through my work with French data (from the end of the 1960s until today), but the bulk of it was acquired when I served as a specialist for the Council of Europe (from 1983 through 2005). These initiatives include the creation and development of the *Council of Europe Annual Penal Statistics (SPACE)*, which I initiated, and particularly the very complex expansion of this system to community measures (*SPACE 2*) at the beginning of the 1990s; participation in the *Sourcebook* program to create a database with all European crime statistics; preparation of the recommendations on prison population inflation and the overcrowding of prisons, adopted on September 20, 1999, by the Committee of Ministers; preparation of the recommendations on conditional release, adopted on September 24, 2003; collaboration within the Criminological Scientific Council in a book addressing "good practices" in criminal justice and correctional policy.[1]

---

[1] Council of Europe. *Crime policy in Europe. Good Practices and Promising Examples* (Strasbourg: Council of Europe Publishing, 2004).

This research on terms and concepts thus led me to create a dictionary of prison demography. What follows are some key entries from this dictionary.[2]

1. Of some concepts

COMMITTAL (ou commitment, peut-être?): Committal is the judicial act whereby a person is placed in a correctional facility, under the responsibility of its director, from a certain date, based on a certain committal order, and on the basis of a given motive (prosecuted or punishable offenses). According to French law, article 432-6 of the penal code states that "the reception or retention of a person by an agent of the prison administration, without a warrant, a judgment or detention order drafted in conformity with the law, or the undue extension of detention, is punished by two years' imprisonment and a fine of €30,000." It is important to distinguish between the committal of a free person and the committal of a person transferred from another correctional facility.

Committal to prison does not imply detention. Such is the case when a convict is placed under electronic surveillance *ab initio*, a form of alternative sanction, introduced in the bill enacted on December 19, 1997. In this case, the person is committed to prison, but not detained.[3]

PENAL DEMOGRAPHY: In practice, there is often no distinction made between *prison demography, correctional demography,* and *penal demography*. It is preferable to use the term *prison demography* to designate the study of carceral populations and the expression *correctional demography* to signify the study of being placed under judicial supervision either in closed containment or in the community. The expression *penal demography* has a much broader meaning and is also sometimes referred to as *criminal demography*. This concept includes the study of all populations involved in the criminal justice system in the broad sense of the term: individuals arrested by the police, brought before the public prosecutor's office, indicted, detained, convicted, incarcerated, etc.

Strictly speaking, prison demography studies the different aspects of prison populations, their criminal and socio-demographic characteristics, their evolution over time, and their spatial distribution. The existence of these populations is essentially regulated by the following basic mechanism:
- individuals are committed and thus become part of the prison population;
- individuals are released, freed, and thus leave this population;
- a certain period of time elapses between a person's committal and release; the time spent in prison, which varies depending on the person, ensures the coexistence, at any moment, of a changing number of individuals that make up the prison population.

Demographic analysis seeks to understand the mechanism by which the population is renewed; for example, we try to identify the connections that exist between the modalities of the committal and release processes (flows) and the number of individuals (stock) that comprise the prison population. This highlights the crucial distinction between stock and flows in this discipline. Prison demography also studies all judiciary, administrative, and human events that might influence the time spent in prison or in detention, as well as the conditions and duration of the detention period.

---

[2] Pierre V. Tournier, *Dictionnaire de démographie pénale. Des outils pour arpenter le champ pénal* (Paris: L'Harmattan, 2010).
[3] See appendix: Data on the committed population on January 1, 2013 (throughout France).

"STOCK-FLOW" EQUATION: Consider an interval of time $[t_0; t_1]$. Let P_0 be the size of the prison population at the initial date t_0 (period start), P_1 the size at date t_1 (period end). Let E be the total number of entries into prison during the period and S the total number of releases during the same period (except for transfers). The "stock-flow" equation is expressed in the following relation: $P_1 = P_0 + E - S$, or $P_1 - P_0 = E - S$. Both express the absolute increase during the period, or the balance.

INDICATOR OF THE AVERAGE TIME SPENT IN PRISON: This indicator can be calculated by comparing the average number of people in prison for year n (P) to the flow of entries into prison for the year (E): $d = 12 \times P/E$ or $P = E \times d/12$ (d expressed in months).

Strictly speaking, this formula corresponds to the demographic model of "stationary population": the number of entries is constant from year to year, with the same release schedule for all cohorts of entries. Of course, prison populations do not generally follow this model. Also, this indicator hardly makes sense in economic terms, but it proves very useful in determining basic trends (hence why I developed this expression in 1981).

EVENT: In the study of the penal system, we are not only interested in populations involved in the criminal justice system, but also in the decisions that occur throughout the criminal justice process (for example, indictment, committal, dismissal, conviction, release) or other issues that impact these decisions (escape, suicide in prison, etc.). We generally seek to identify the number of *events*, usually over a calendar year (flow), and their relative frequency. The frequency is calculated by creating a ratio of the number of events in a year to the population that is susceptible to experiencing that event (rate): rate of entries to prison or detention per population size, and rates of mortality or suicide in prison. We are also interested in the time lapsed between two events.

Among all these events, we make a distinction between those that are *renewable*, that can happen again during the lifetime of a single person (e.g., new convictions for acts committed after release), and those that are not renewable (e.g., death, conviction for the first acts committed after release).

2. Two major variables: the nature of the offense and the penal category

In general demography, the most important variables are, for obvious reasons, sex and age. Unsurprisingly, in the field of penal demography, the nature of the offense and the penal category are central variables. These two variables are particularly complex to analyze, both judicially and statistically. Sex and age also relate to the sociological dimension of the penal field but at a secondary level, as do family situation, foreign origin, nationality and origin, education, profession or work situation, health, addictive behaviors, etc.

OFFENSE: In French law, criminal offenses are classified, according to their seriousness, as *felonies, misdemeanors,* or *petty offenses* (art. 111-1 of the Penal Code). Petty offenses are subdivided into five classes. With regard to felonies, the maximum penalty—*criminal imprisonment (ordinary offenses) or criminal detention (political or military offenses)*—is life imprisonment. For misdemeanors, the maximum penalty is 10 years imprisonment. Penalties for petty offenses include fines (a maximum of 1500 euros for fifth-class offenses and in some cases, 3000 euros for repeat offenders) and the forfeiture or restriction of rights, as indicated in article 131-14 of the Penal Code. Since the new penal code was adopted on March 1, 1994, penalties entailing the deprivation of liberty can no longer be applied to fifth-class petty offenses.

Of the 603,994 convictions registered in the criminal records in 2011, there were 2,529 felonies (0.4%), 560,259 misdemeanors (93%), and 41,206 fifth-class petty offenses (6.8%). Of the felonies, 50% of the convictions involved incidents of rape. As for misdemeanors, drunk driving was the most prevalent (22%), followed by intentional assault and battery with temporary interruption of work (TIW) for eight days or less, with aggravating circumstances (8%). Fifth-class petty offenses primarily consist of incidents of excessive speeding (35%) and intentional assault and battery with TIW for eight days or less (22%).[4]

MULTIPLE OFFENSES: A prison sentence may be linked to multiple cases, and each case could originate from a different offense. However, even within a single case, there might also be several indictable or punishable offenses. A conviction, for example, might include rape, threat of death, and robbery. If, when looking at a group of convictions, the aim is to determine the statistical distribution according to the type of punishable offenses, it is tempting to try to simplify things by basing the analysis on the concept of *primary offense*. In a certain number of cases, the definition is straightforward. If the conviction involves a felony and misdemeanors, the felony would be designated as the primary offense. In the case of several felonies (or several misdemeanors), the felony (or the misdemeanor) with the heaviest sentence, as defined by the penal code, would be designated as the primary offense.

Example 1. Rape (punishable by 15 years imprisonment, art. 222-23 of the Penal Code) and robbery (3 years imprisonment and 45,000 euros, art. 311-3). Primary offense = rape.

Example 2. Death threat with an order to fulfill a condition (punished by 5 years' imprisonment and 75,000 euros, art 22-18) and robbery. Primary offense = threat of death with an order to fulfill a condition.

But this approach has its limits.

Example 3. Death threat (3 years' imprisonment and 45,000 euros, art. 222-17) and robbery. Primary offense = ?

The rationale may be that harm done to individuals outweighs harm targeted at goods. It is also possible to have felonies (or misdemeanors) of the same type with similar sentences. Thus, when looking at two offenses, it is not always possible to determine which one is more serious than the other, based solely on the prescribed sentence. According to statistical sources and studies, this problem can be resolved in a practical way, and the primary offense can be determined on the basis of which offense is mentioned first in the concerned document (committal document, memorial of judgment, etc.).

PENAL CATEGORY: At a period *t*, the prison population comprises defendants and inmates. An inmate is an incarcerated individual who has been convicted and received a final ruling: the person must have exhausted his/her judicial remedies (appeal and cross-appeal). However, the additional appeal time available to the prosecution is not taken into account. A distinction is also made between inmates serving a sentence of imprisonment

---

[4]O. Timbart, *Les condamnations, année 2011*. Secrétariat général du Ministère de la Justice et des Libertés (Paris: SDSE, 2013).

and those serving a term of imprisonment or criminal detention for either a fixed or life term.

Defendants are individuals in prison who have not received a final ruling, who are in pretrial detention. They may be subject to proceedings involving a misdemeanor or a crime. They may be awaiting a preliminary ruling or have already received an initial ruling.

If the person is involved in several cases, the status of inmate takes precedence over the status of defendant. The penal category is determined at a particular moment in time and may, of course, change during the period of detention; this is a characteristic of stock.

PENAL CATEGORY AT PRISON ENTRY: When entering prison, a person has the status of defendant or inmate. Inmates are individuals imprisoned after a final ruling, while defendants, defined in negative terms, are those who have not yet received a final ruling.

CHRONOLOGICAL PENAL CATEGORY: This concept only has meaning once the prison term has been completed. Penal status is attributed to the time spent in prison on the basis of the imprisoned person's penal category, either defendant or inmate. Time spent in prison is thus broken down into the length of time spent in pre-trial detention and length of time spent as an inmate. One of these factors of course may be null for any given time spent in prison. Also, when a person is required to remain in prison over a period of time for multiple cases, this breakdown necessarily involves making prioritized choices. Let us look at an example:

- January 1, 2005: Committal to prison of Victor D. under a committal order for rape in case 1.
- March 1, 2005: Memorial of judgment in case 2. One year imprisonment for petty theft. Credit towards a reduced sentence of 3 months, with a sentence end date of December 1, 2005.
- December 1, 2005: End of sentence in case 2. Victor D is held in detention due to the committal order in case 1.
- April 1, 2006: Judgment by the Assize Court in case 1 results in the acquittal and release of Victor D.

Between March 1 and December 1 (9 months), the status of inmate (in case 2) takes precedence over that of defendant in case 1. The breakdown of this detention of a year and three months based on the chronological penal category is the following: detention as a defendant = 6 months (or 40%), detention as an inmate = 9 months (or 60%).

This concept of chronological penal category should be distinguished from that of penal category on date t. Let us look at a second example:

- January 1, 2005: Committal to prison of Clara H. under a committal order for robbery and driving without a license.
- March 1, 2005: Order to send the case to the criminal court.
- June 1, 2005: Judgment by the criminal court. Clara H. is sentenced to 18 months' imprisonment, of which six months were suspended. Three months' credit for a reduced sentence. End of sentence: October 1, 2005.
- October 1, 2005: Release from prison; end of sentence.

Here is the breakdown of the 9 months, done a posteriori: time spent as a defendant = 5 months (or 56%); time spent as an inmate = 4 months (or 44%). We know that at the end of the time spent in prison, Clara H. did not appeal the criminal court's decision. Thus, a posteriori the conviction became final as of June 1. In reality, Clara H. held the status of defendant longer. If we ask what her penal category was in the days following the June 1 ruling, the answer is "defendant," because she was still in the period where she could lodge an appeal or give notice of appeal.

In a now dated study,[5] based on a sample of entering inmates from 1983 who were followed for up to 27 months (enough time for more than 95% of entering inmates to be released), the breakdown of time spent in prison was as follows: time in prison as a defendant = 50.1%, time spent as an inmate = 49.9%. This type of calculation, which did not include the 5% of inmates who spent more than 27 months in prison, has not been replicated since the publication of this study.

3. Calculation of rates

RATES: The quantitative approach in the correctional field obviously involves manipulating several *rates*: rate of population increase, rate of detainee supervision (per correctional officer), rate of individuals in prison per inhabitant, rate of detention per inhabitant, rate of entries into prison per inhabitant, rate of entries into detention per inhabitant, rate of mortality in prison, etc. Note that in related situations, the following terms are also used: *proportion* (e.g., the proportion of individuals in pretrial detention), *index* (specific frequency index of a sanction or measure applied in the community), *weight* (weight of the temporary detention, weight of alternatives to detention), and quotient (quotient of recidivism). In each case, the aim is to calculate a ratio of two quantities, *A* and *B*; however, the relationships that exist between these two figures may be different in kind.

First case. In this case, the goal is to measure the relative frequency of an event in a given population, generally throughout a calendar year, whether the event is renewable or not. The number of events (*A*) is thus compared to the average population that might experience this event (*B*). The relative frequency of a non-renewable event could be considered as an experimental measure of the likelihood of its occurrence. This is how the prison mortality rate is calculated.

Second case. This case involves the division of a part by the whole. *A* and *B* are of the same kind (persons or events) and *A* is a part of *B*. In this case, the preferable term to use is *proportion* or *weight*. Some examples are the proportion of women or foreigners in the prison population (these are also commonly referred to as the rate of women or the rate of individuals of foreign origin), the proportion of individuals in prison not yet tried (*A* and *B* are individuals in prison), the proportion of entries into prison before a final ruling (*A* and *B* are "entries into prison" events), and the weight of detention alternatives.

Third case. The dividend and the divisor belong to different categories. This is the case for the rate of detainee supervision (per correctional officer), where *A* is a number of detainees and *B* a number of officers, and for the specific frequency index of a community sanction or measure. This case is also known as a *ratio*.

In what category do we place the clearance rate found in statistics concerning incidents reported by the police and the gendarmerie (relating the number of reported incidents to cleared incidents from the same year)? Neither case 1 nor case 2 applies in this example. Indeed, the cleared incidents from year *n* are not a sub-group of reported incidents from the same year, since some of these clearances may have resulted from proceedings from a

---

[5]Marie Danièle Barré, Pierre V. Tournier, and Bessie Leconte. *La mesure du temps carcéral, observation suivie d'une cohorte d'entrants* (Paris: CESDIP, 1988).

previous year. This is, therefore, a simple ratio, which for certain offenses may be greater than 100.

Relating, in a mathematical sense, one quantity (*A*) to another (*B*) is one of the first stages of analysis. The meaning of the operation will obviously depend on the types of quantities.

4. The stories of cohorts

COHORT: A cohort is any group of persons who experience the same event within a given time frame, usually a calendar year. Demography's traditional cohorts (cohorts of births, of generations, or of deaths, etc.) give way to cohorts of individuals committed to prison or detained, cohorts of persons benefiting from a release, etc. Whether it involves observation over time (e.g., observation of cohorts of people committed to prison) or retrospective analysis (e.g., of cohorts of those released), the value of this kind of approach can be explained in this way: "The fact is that biographical events do not occur according to clear groups, only to be lost in a mass of statistics. On the contrary, these events are submitted to the analyst as individual stories, which allow for particularly rich analyses due to the network of connections that can be brought out between the different types of events at play."[6] Even if this approach is not the prerogative of demographers, it has greatly contributed to the visibility of our way of understanding the correctional field. In our work, analyses of cohorts have primarily focused on the three following areas, which are more or less interwoven: the study of incarceration trends and trajectories and the lengths of time spent in prison, early release and alternative sanctions and finally, the issue of "recidivism."

LONGITUDINAL ANALYSIS: This expression is synonymous with analysis by cohort. Observations over time (prospective analysis) and retrospective analysis are the two main methods employed to collect longitudinal data. It is fundamentally different from cross-sectional analysis.[7]

RETROSPECTIVE COHORT ANALYSIS: As its title indicates, retrospective cohort analysis is a return to the past. Here is an example: to study changes and trends in early release decisions, we use cohorts of inmates freed during a certain period, and we examine, retrospectively, the decisions that affected them throughout their time in prison—convictions, credits toward reduced sentences, possible withdrawal of those reduced sentences after particular incidents, anticipated conditions of release, etc. We are thus able to reconstitute a history of the time in prison.

In this type of research, the study of modified sentences and early releases are usually combined with the study of "recidivism."[8] The retrospective analysis of what occurred before release (during the time in prison, or even before that period) includes the observation over time of what occurs afterwards (new cases).

---

[6] R. Pressat, *Dictionnaire de démographie* (Paris: PUF, 1979).

[7] Pierre V. Tournier, "Note technique sur le diagramme de Lexis," in *Travaux & Documents*, 2 (Paris: Direction de l'administration pénitentiaire, 1980).

[8] A. Kensey and Pierre V. Tournier. "Prisonniers du passé? Cohorte des personnes condamnées libérées en 1996–1997: examen de leur casier judiciaire 5 ans après la levée d'écrou (échantillon national aléatoire stratifié selon l'infraction)," in *Travaux & Documents*, 68 (Paris: Direction de l'administration pénitentiaire, 2005).

CROSS-SECTIONAL ANALYSIS: cross-sectional analysis involves phenomena that appear during a set period of time, usually a calendar year, within a set of cohorts.[9] It is fundamentally different from longitudinal analysis. Here is an example: consider a cohort of persons committed to prison. Through observation over time, we can learn who among the inmates of this cohort will benefit from temporary leave during their detention. This follow-up can persist up until their release. By ranking these leaves (1st leave, 2nd, etc.), we can analyze the conditions under which these leaves took place (without incident, late return to the detention facility, escape). This would be a longitudinal analysis.

However, in a cross-sectional study, we might also look at all the leaves granted in a particular year to the population of convicted detainees. These detainees would belong to an entirely different set of imprisoned cohorts and would represent a heterogeneous population with regard to the length of time already spent in prison.

OBSERVATION OVER TIME: Unlike *retrospective cohort analysis,* which looks to the past, the *observation of a cohort over time* looks toward the future. As an example, let us look at one of the first correctional studies carried out in France using this method. It involved the 6,745 entries into detention in February 1983.[10] In cases where one person entered several times, only the first entry of the month was considered. Thus, we can in fact refer to them as *incoming inmates.* The study began in 1983 and involved three periods.

During the first period, we analyzed the socio-demographic and criminal structure of this cohort. After determining a representative sample of these incoming inmates (n=1326), we allowed for a sufficient period of time to pass so that most incoming inmates were released. Following a few tests, we decided to end this period of observation after 27 months: 95% of the incoming inmates had been released at that point. Fifty percent had been released after 2.5 months (median of the duration of detention). It was then possible to analyze the time spent in prison: the schedule of exits, the study of detention, of pre-trial detention and of (short) sentence modification.

The third step of the observation over time involved examining the individual criminal records of the sample, on average five years after release. For those released before a ruling was issued, it was possible to determine whether they had ultimately been convicted and if so, of the nature of the sentence. For all cases, we could determine whether they had been involved in a new offense after their release, and whether they were convicted (study of the cohort's judicial follow-up). Fifty-nine percent of those released were involved in a new case, punishable by a penalty of some kind, and the rate of return to prison was 39%.

5. Prison population inflation and overpopulation of prisons

PRISON POPULATION INFLATION: Any mention of prison population inflation suggests that the increase in the number of persons in prison is "very high" (stock data). In other words, it does not correspond with the increase in the number of inhabitants.[11]

---

[9] Tournier, "Note technique."

[10] Barré, Tournier, and Leconte, La mesure.

[11] Council of Europe. *Prison overcrowding and prison population inflation,* recommendation No. R (99) 22, adopted by the Committee of Ministers on September 30, 1999, and report prepared with

Example: In France, between January 1, 1975, and January 1, 1995, the number of persons in prison became 1.98 times higher, an increase of 98% compared to only a 10.3% increase in the number of inhabitants (metropolitan France). Thus, in 20 years, the rate of incarcerated individuals, which can be calculated based on a constant number of inhabitants, went from 49 to 89 per 100,000 inhabitants. Looking at things this way, we can assess the magnitude of the increase in the prison population rate, without having to address issues of causality (i.e., is it because of the increase and structural transformation of crime and criminality? Or the increased severity of trial courts?), and without having to refer to issues relating to the capacity of detention facilities.

The concept of prison population inflation (which only makes when observing over a sufficiently long interval of time such that changes are not merely circumstantial) is distinct from the concept of overpopulation of detention facilities. Overpopulation only involves detained persons and refers to the situation on a given date *t*.

If the number of incarcerated individuals decreases significantly over a certain period of time, this would indicate prison deflation. This was the case in France between 1996 and 2000. Again, as previously mentioned, it is important to make a distinction within the prison population between those individuals in prison who are detained and those in prison who are not detained.

PRISON OVERPOPULATION: In everyday language, this expression has two fairly distinct meanings: (A) A general sense that "there are too many detainees," without any indication of what criteria are being used to make this claim; (B) a more precise meaning referring to the capacity of detention facilities. This second meaning describes the fact that, at a given moment *t*, the number of detainees does not correspond to the detention facilities' capacity. Overpopulation is thus evaluated according to prison density and the surplus number of detainees. It is important to make a distinction between overpopulation and the inflation of the number of individuals in prison, or even of the number of persons detained. For example, there could be an increase in overpopulation while the number of detainees remains constant (and therefore no inflation). This would occur, for example, with the closure of a dilapidated facility, the conversion of cells into workshops, etc. Of course, overpopulation and prison inflation are usually linked, but this link can be complex. If there is not enough construction, inflation increases the problem of overpopulation. Yet, does overpopulation mobilize public authorities to decrease inflation by decreasing the use of prisons? Does under-population (which occurs when policies to develop prison buildings are poorly conceived) encourage inflation? Because of the lack of research in this area, we cannot speak with certainty and are compelled to hypothesize. However, it should be noted that making a distinction between the two concepts at least enables us to consider the ways in which they are connected.[12]

NUMBER OF SURPLUS DETAINEES: This indicator is crucial for measuring the state of prison overpopulation.[13] Let us consider two detention facilities *A* and *B*. On date *t*, *A* has 100 functional spaces and *B* has 150, for a total of 250 spaces.

---

the assistance of André Kuhn, Pierre V. Tournier and Roy Walmsley, et al. (Strasbourg: Council of Europe Publishing, 2000).

[12] Council of Europe, *Prison overcrowding*.

[13] Pierre V. Tournier, *La Prison. Une nécessité pour la République* (Paris: Les Editions Buchet & Chastel, 2013).

First case. *A* receives 120 detainees and *B* 180 detainees. Overall, there are 300 detainees for 250 spaces, a difference of 50. There is a surplus of 20 detainees in *A* and a surplus of 30 detainees in *B* (20 + 30 = 50). The total number of surplus detainees corresponds to the positive difference between the total number of detainees and the total number of spaces.

Second case. *A* receives 80 detainees and *B* 110 detainees. Overall, there are 190 detainees for 250 spaces, a difference of –60. There are 20 free spaces in *A* and 40 free spaces in *B* (20 + 40 = 60). The total number of free spaces corresponds to the difference (negative) between the total number of detainees and the total number of spaces.

Third case. *A* receives 80 detainees and *B* 180 detainees. Overall, there are 260 detainees for 250 spaces, a difference of + 10 (apparent overpopulation). In reality, there are 20 free spaces in *A* and 30 surplus detainees in *B*, for an overall number of surplus detainees of 30. The difference, positive in this case, between the total number of detainees and the total number of spaces does indeed indicate a state of overpopulation, but does not measure the number of surplus detainees.

Surplus detainees = apparent overpopulation + number of free spaces (30 = 10 + 20).

Fourth case. *A* receives 110 detainees and *B* 120 detainees. Overall, there are 230 detainees for 250 spaces, a difference of –20 (apparent under-population). In reality, there are 10 surplus detainees in *A* and 30 free spaces in *B*, for a total number of surplus detainees of 10. The negative difference between the total number of detainees and the total number of spaces simply indicates that not all the facilities are overpopulated.

Surplus detainees = apparent overpopulation + number of free spaces. (10 = –20 + 30)

6. Should we limit the use of prison?

DYNAMIC TYPOLOGY OF ALTERNATIVE MEASURES AND PENAL SANCTIONS TO PRISON AND/OR DETENTION: It was after work done for the Council of Europe's Council for Penological Co-operation on the overpopulation of detention facilities and prison population inflation that we proposed an original typology of alternatives to prison and/or detention.[14] This classification is based on an analysis of the ways in which the prison population is renewed (individuals in prison): Analysis of stock based on that of entries into prison and length of time spent in prison.

A first-category alternative is any measure or penal sanction (MPS) that reduces the number of entries into prison. Such is the case when, during proceedings, a free defendant is given a suspended sentence or a suspended sentence with probation and is placed under court supervision *ab initio* (decided before any pre-trial detention) or given community service. These alternatives are sometimes regarded as radical.

Second-category alternatives reduce the length of time spent in prison. This is a measure of lesser evil since it is partial or relative: Recourse to prison could not be avoided, but time spent in prison is reduced by some means. Accordingly, reductions of sentences are second-category alternatives.

Of course, this dichotomy does not mean we can classify all MPSs into two separate categories since many belong to one or the other depending on how they were applied.

---

[14] Council of Europe, *Prison overcrowding*.

Thus, court supervision is a first-category measure if it is declared *ab initio*. But if the decision is reached while the defendant is in pre-trial detention, it is a second-category measure: it reduces the time spent in prison while awaiting judgment. It is the same with suspended sentences: it is a first-category sanction if the accused was not in temporary detention, and a second-category sanction in the opposite case. Conditional release (CR) falls into the second category. Of course it does not reduce the time served for the sentence, but it does enable anticipated release—with discharge from prison—with the remainder of the sentence to be served in open custody. Thus, questions concerning early release decisions are an integral part of the issues surrounding alternative sanctions.

The limitations of the preceding dichotomy within the group of alternative sanctions are thus clearly evident. What then, for example, of inmates placed under electronic surveillance? This would not fall under the first category, because the person is committed to prison. Nor does it fall under the second category, because it does not reduce the amount of time spent in prison. Thus, third-category alternatives are MPSs that reduce the real time spent behind the walls of detention facilities, without discharge, and thus without reducing the time spent in prison. This third category therefore includes measures such as electronically monitored house arrest, for which the person committed to prison is not detained, in the sense of being housed in a detention facility. But we can also find measures where the person is housed, but whose time spent behind walls is reduced in some way: semi-custody, extra-mural placement with housing, leave of absence.

As argued in the recommendations put forth by the Council of Europe in 1999, the best way to combat prison inflation is to develop, simultaneously, the three types of alternatives.[15]

VIRTUAL ALTERNATIVES TO PRISON AND/OR TO DETENTION: When a person, who has not yet been subjected to pretrial detention, is placed under court supervision *ab initio* and later receives a simple suspended sentence (total), it might seem that this individual supervision measure effectively allowed this person to escape from prison. However, one could also suggest that the judge would not have made use of pretrial detention if court supervision had not existed in law. The judge used an additional guarantee. If this is the case, court supervision is not serving as an alternative to detention, but is instead a virtual alternative. As a consequence, it *widens the net of social control*; this is the theory of *net-widening*. This same question can, in fact, be raised for all first-category alternatives. Would an offender sentenced to public service have received a fixed prison term if public service were not included in the range of penalties? Would the offender not have rather *benefited* from a suspended sentence, or even from a fine?

In the realm of second-category alternatives, the matter is quite different. An offender who still has three years of solitary confinement to complete, and who receives conditional release (CR), benefits from a real alternative. He will complete the remaining three years of his sentence outside prison walls. And yet...

In France, CRs are uncommon. Suppose that this measure were one day more commonly used. Would it not lead to a compensatory increase in the number of sentences handed down by jurisdictions frustrated by the *erosion* of *their* sanctions? Thus, a very

---

[15] Council of Europe, *Prison overcrowding*.

real "micro" second category alternative, which clearly benefits the offender, might become virtual at the "macro" level.[16]

7. Foretelling the future?

POPULATION PERSPECTIVE: Similar terms also used are *projection* or *forecast.*[17] Projection refers to calculations regarding a population's future evolution based on certain hypotheses that are not necessarily plausible. This is generally the case when calculating the amount of time required for a population to double. We simply look at the consequences a change may have on the rate of relative annual constant increase over a period of time.

When the hypotheses are more or less plausible, we then speak of perspective. The term "forecast" is only used when the hypotheses upon which they are based appear very probable.

In addition, there are distinctions between *descriptive* and *explanatory* perspective models. At the beginning of the 1980s (2), Marie Danièle Barré and I used a very simple descriptive model to study the prison population, using only time to explain changes in trends. This model is based on the linear extrapolation of past tendencies (chronological series) and the consideration of the prison population's seasonal variations (stocks on the first day of the month). For instance, using the prison population on December 31, 2005, this technique makes it possible to estimate the number of individuals in prison on the first day of each month in 2006 and 2007 (unless there are "disruptive phenomena" not taken into account in the calculation). Thus on that date, we might suppose, but without any certainty, that there will be an amnesty after the presidential election in May 2007; it is simply a tradition of the Republic and nothing requires Parliament to make such a law. This is the first uncertainty. The second uncertainty is that, if there is a vote, this law may be more or less lenient and may therefore have a greater or lesser effect on the prison population. A third uncertainty is whether the law will be combined with a collective pardon. While these calculations cannot claim to "foretell" and require frequent adjustments, they do show the numerical consequences of a simple hypothesis: if changes continue according to the trend of recent years, where are we headed? They are also a good economic tool, allowing calculations to be made for budgetary purposes, monthly statistics to be put into perspective (taking seasonal variations and so on into account), and the effects of an amnesty or collective pardon to be measured. Nonetheless, the model we introduced in 1979 has since been taken up for the study of correctional administration and seems to have been of some use.

Explanatory models are much more ambitious.[18] They can be either *mechanistic* or *theoretical*. In the first case, the formation process of the prison population is broken down into its different stages: crime submitted to the court, crime prosecuted, crime

---

[16] Pierre V. Tournier, "Real Alternatives Versus Virtual Alternatives: On the Theory of Net-Widening Applied to Electronic Monitoring in France," in *Will Electronic Monitoring Have a Future in Europe?* eds M. Mayer, R. Haverkamp, and R. Lévy (Freiburg: Max Planck Institute, 2003), 177-186.

[17] Louis Henry. *Dictionnaire démographique multilingue, volume français* (Liège: Ordinal Editions, 1981).

[18] Marie Danièle Barré. "Résistible progression des effectifs de la population carcérale en France? Réflexion sur les projections." Paper presented at the 8th National Demographic Colloquium, Grenoble, France, 1987.

penalized by being committed to prison. Without attempting to explain the stages, we measure them and their sequence based on a perspective of the affected population, ending with the provisional number of persons in prison. With a theoretical model, we empirically verify a hypothesis concerning the role of a certain number of variables (unemployment, the level of urbanization, etc.) in the crime and consequently in the prison population.

This poses a two-fold problem: the model does not adapt well to perspective because it requires perspectives on explanatory variables to be used; it brings variables into play that are difficult to act on over the short or medium term.[19]

***

This contribution to the journal, *Criminology,* is potentially the first stage of a larger project I envisioned when I published my prison demography dictionary in French in 2000. I hope to leverage the skills needed in order to present the most important terms and concepts of that work in several languages (English, German and Spanish). Dealing with language will clearly play an important role in this kind of approach, and not just in terms of translation. It will also be necessary to consider how to transfer concepts. The most obvious example is the word "probation," which, in English, encompasses very different penalties, depending on the country.[20] In England or Wales, as well as in Sweden and Denmark, "probation" suggests an "autonomous penalty after being found guilty, without a sentence entailing the deprivation of liberty." "Probation" in France refers to a suspended prison sentence (with a defined quantum). The suspension might be total or partial. At the Council of Europe, the word "probation" is used in a general sense to indicate the enforcement of a penalty or measure applied in any community.[21] Thus, if we are not careful, there is considerable risk of confusion in international comparisons.

Paris, March 19, 2013.

---

[19] Home Office. *International Seminar on Prison Population Projections, Report of Proceedings.* Vol. 1–2. Shrigley Hall, July 9–11, 1991.

Pierre V. Tournier, "Godot is Arrived. When French Parliament at the End Vote the Promised Prison Law," in *Punitivity: International Developments,* eds. H. Helmuth Kury, and E. Shea (Hagen, Germany: Universitätsverlag Dr. N. Brockmeyer, Vol. II, 2011), 551-584.

Tournier, *La Prison.*

[20] Tournier, *La Prison.*

[21] According to the Council of Europe's terminology, community sanctions and measures (CSM) are penalties and measures besides detention, and are combined with "supervision" measures, that is, measures for support, assistance, and supervision.

References

Barré, Marie Danièle. 1987. "Résistible progression des effectifs de la population carcérale en France? Réflexion sur les projections." Paper presented at the 8th National Demographic Colloquium, Grenoble, France.

Barré, Marie Danièle, Pierre V. Tournier, and Bessie Leconte. 1988. *La mesure du temps carcéral, observation suivie d'une cohorte d'entrants*. Paris: CESDIP.

Council of Europe. 2000. *Prison overcrowding and prison population inflation*. Recommendation No. R (99) 22, adopted by the Committee of Ministers on September 30, 1999, and report prepared with the assistance of André Kuhn, Pierre V. Tournier and Roy Walmsley, et al. Strasbourg: Council of Europe Publishing.

Council of Europe. 2004. *Crime Policy in Europe. Good Practices and Promising Examples*. Strasbourg: Council of Europe Publishing.

Henry, Louis. 1981. *Dictionnaire démographique multilingue, volume français*. Liège: Ordinal Editions.

Home Office. 1991. *International Seminar on Prison Population Projections, Report of Proceedings*. Vol. 1–2. Shrigley Hall, July 9–11.

Kensey, A., and Pierre V. Tournier. 2005. "Prisonniers du passé? Cohorte des personnes condamnées libérées en 1996–1997: examen de leur casier judiciaire 5 ans après la levée d'écrou (échantillon national aléatoire stratifié selon l'infraction)." In *Travaux & Documents*, 68. Paris: Direction de l'administration pénitentiaire.

Pressat, R. 1979. *Dictionnaire de démographie*. Paris: PUF.

Timbart, O. 2013. *Les condamnations, année 2011*. Secrétariat général du Ministère de la Justice et des Libertés. February 2013. Paris: SDSE.

Tournier, Pierre V. 1980. "Note technique sur le diagramme de Lexis." In *Travaux & Documents*, 2. Paris: Direction de l'administration pénitentiaire.

Tournier, Pierre V. 2003. "Real Alternatives versus Virtual Alternatives: On the Theory of Net-Widening Applied to Electronic Monitoring in France." In *Will Electronic Monitoring Have a Future in Europe?* Eds. by M. Mayer, R. Haverkamp, and R. Lévy. Freiburg: Max Planck Institute, 177-186.

Tournier, Pierre V. 2010. *Dictionnaire de démographie pénale. Des outils pour arpenter le champ pénal*. Paris: L'Harmattan.

Tournier, Pierre V. 2011. "Godot is Arrived. When French Parliament at the End Vote the Promised Prison Law." In *Punitivity: International Developments*, eds H. Helmuth Kury, and E. Shea, Vol. 2. Hagen, Germany: Universitätsverlag Dr. N. Brockmeyer, 551-584.

Tournier, Pierre V. 2013. *La Prison. Une nécessité pour la République*. Paris: Les Editions Buchet & Chastel.

Appendix

Population held in custody on January 1, 2013 (France as a whole)
* Based on data supplied by the Correctional Administration

On January 1, 2013, 76,798 were under correctional control in France: 16,454 individuals were in pretrial detention, 50,118 individuals were convicted and incarcerated (for a total of 66,572 detained individuals), 9,653 individuals were placed under electronic surveillance (9,029 individuals through early release, 624 individuals via an end-of-sentence parole condition), and 573 individuals in extra-mural placements, without prison housing. The rate of committal to prison was 117 per 100,000 inhabitants, and the detention rate was 102 per 100,000 inhabitants.

The rate of defendants among the persons in prison was 21%. It was 25% compared to the detained population.

Twenty percent of inmates in prison have received a modified sentence, in prison (partial release, electronic surveillance, extra-mural placement with or without detention housing). This indicator does not take account of the 624 inmates placed under electronically monitored house arrest at the end of their sentence (application of the penal law dated November 24, 2009).

The number of minors detained is 724. Of them, 261 (or 36%) are in facilities for minors. These facilities are under-occupied (348 functional spaces, of which 87 are unoccupied).

Change over the last 12 months

The number of individuals in prison has increased over 12 months (3,018 more persons in prison, an annual rate of increase of +4.1%). The number reached on January 1, 2003 [2013?] (76,798) was less than the record high reached on July 1, 2012 (78,262). The annual growth rate has been decreasing for a year: 10.2% on January 1, 2012, 7.9% on April 1, 6.7% on July 1, 5.6% on October 1, 4.1% on January 1, 2013.

The number of detainees is also increasing (1,785 more detainees during the previous 12 months, an annual rate of increase of + 2.8%). The number reached on January 1, 2013 (66,572) was less than the record high reached on December 1 (67,674). The annual rate of increase has been decreasing for a year: 7.0% on January 1, 2012, 4.7% on April 1, 4.1% on July 1, 4.0% on October 1, 2.8% on January 1, 2013.

The number of minors detained has increased slightly (12 fewer detainees over the last 12 months, an annual rate of increase of + 1.7%).

Overpopulation

Over the previous 12 months, the number of functional spaces in detention went from 57,236 to 56,992 (244 fewer spaces in a year, an annual rate of increase of –0.4%). The number of surplus detainees is 12,194. This is an increase from a year ago (11,251 12 months ago, or 943 more, for an annual rate of increase of +8.4%). This indicator measures the state of overpopulation by taking account of each facility's situation, and of each section in detention centers. During the "2004–2012" period, the maximum was noted on June 1, 2004 with a number of surplus detainees of 16,086. The minimum was noted on August 1, 2006, with a surplus number of detainees of 7,717. The number of detainees sleeping on a mat on the floor is 639 as of January 1, 2013.

Annual entries into prison and indicator of the average duration of time in prison

In 2011, the increase in the average number of persons in prison was linked to an increase in the number of entries into prison, which was 6.4% higher compared to 2010 (88,058 versus 82,725). The indicator of the average duration of time spent in prison remained stable, but at a record level (9.8 months).

Field: The whole of France

	2006	2007	2008	2009	2010	2011
Annual entries into prison (E)	86,594	90,270	89,054	84,355	82,725	88,058
Average population in prison (P) (i)	59,938	63,268	66,716	67,362	67,317	71,755
Average duration in prison (d, in months) (ii)	8.3 m	8.4 m	9.0 m	9.6 m	9.8 m	9.8 m

(i) Average of the numbers on the first day of each month.

(ii) This indicator of average time spent in prison (d) is calculated according to the equation $P = E \times d$ (where P is the average number throughout the year and E is the number of committals to prison in the year), an equation based on the hypothesis of stationarity (constant annual committals to prison, with identical release schedules for all imprisoned cohorts).

About the Author
Pierre V. Tournier serves as Research Director at CNRS, 20th Century Social History Center (Université Paris 1),://pierre-victortournier.blogspot.fr/

Competition Between Those Involved in Public Debate on Crime Statistics: Formalization and Case Studies Based on Direct Experience

Cyril Rizk & Christophe Soullez

Abstract:
Competitive relationships in the public debate on crime statistics: Theoretical approach and case studies from self-experience

The creation in France in 2003 of the OND[1] was the opportunity for the public statistics system to extend its presence in the field of crime statistics, as previously, it was limited to judicial statistics only. At the end of 2004, it distributed figures relating to incidents recorded by police and gendarmes. According to new methodology and with the launch, alongside INSEE in 2007 of an annual initiative of national victimization studies, the ONDRP has become one of the "producers" of official statistics on crime.

We put ourselves forward to interpret the actions, interactions, and reactions that this process led to in a formal framework that we call "competition between those involved in public debate". Two case studies are presented, one on competition within official statistics between the OND and institutional communication of the ministry of the interior, and on the other hand, competition between researchers among the first to introduce victimization studies in France in the 1980s.

KEY WORDS: *public debate, competition, official statistics, police recorded crime, victimization surveys*
Geographical index: France
Chronological index: 21st century

Since 2004, the date of the creation of the ONDRP, that is to say the national structure responsible for analysis and distribution of data on crime and criminality, debates were started in the scientific community regarding the relevance of the use of administrative statistics on crime in public debate. Some universities, but also some parliamentarians, were interested in how the ONDRP ensures the mission of analysis, production, and distribution of crime statistics.

Many articles have been written on the development of the ONDRP (Ocqueteau 2012), and its presence which is increasingly visible in the sphere of the media and politics, and in certain methodology studies (Mouhanna 2007; 2008).

The ONDRP has also sometimes been criticized for its status and in particular its position within the administration (initially associated as a public administrative establishment under the supervision of the prime minister) with the question of its independence regarding services producing data.

Up until 2004, the analysis of criminal statistics lay in the hands of a small community of scientists and the commentary and distribution was the sole responsibility of the ministry of the interior.

---

[1] The National supervisory body on crime.

It is in this context that the ONDRP had to deal with, or one might say, face up to, these two protagonists while also ensuring it carried out its role as distributer of statistical information and, therefore, ultimately as a contributor to public debate.

Nowadays, the ONDRP attracts attention, in particular from people who, logically, are outside of the process of designing, collecting, processing, analyzing, and producing data and are therefore not at the centre of interactions, struggles of influence or in more mundane terms, means of cooperation with data producing services. It therefore seemed useful to us, its main partners, to offer a theoretical framework capable of explaining certain episodes which have taken place since its creation.

Concerned about transparency, the ONDRP has always preferred to say that in statistics, it is important to realize that its work is subjective and that this is an inherent part of work on figures, rather than deluding oneself with the illusion of remaining objective.

Accepting that this work is subjective means that we make a distinction between the choices which can be made in a mathematical way and those which are partly, and necessarily, discretional.

This margin for manoeuvre is not usually updated in publications on statistics: the ONDRP has taken on the duty of exposing it as clearly as possible. They explain their choices in a detailed way, by specifying the degree to which they are subjective. In particular, it is a question of reminding people that the options which are chosen are not always the only possibilities.

Following the same principle of transparency, we suggest a thorough re-reading of events which needs to be both well-structured in terms of argument, and documented, but which never is considered as the only possible interpretation. It is a question of trying to remain convincing, despite the handicap of the absence of distance from the object of analysis. Furthermore, it would not make sense that only those who are outside the process, and therefore also without practical knowledge of the work carried out, are the only ones able to express themselves.

In this particular case, this article does not intend to deal with issues raised by the mechanisms for producing knowledge of an organization such as the ONDRP. It does not focus on relations between the ONDRP and the media either. Instead, it aims for an approach where two partners use each other mutually or use, via the main administration, methodology advocated by the ONDRP.

It puts forward, with two concrete examples, a demonstration of difficulties for a new service of studies to impose itself in public debate. It is faced with two categories of different organizations: sociologists, from the centre of sociological research on law and institutions working on criminal issues (the CESDIP) at the heart of the first national victimization study which considers itself as having the monopoly over statistical interpretation, in this field, and the administration which took over almost all the institutional communication on the état 4001, tool for recording crimes and offences recorded by the police and national gendarmerie.

Statistics as part of public debate

All those who participate in public debate regarding statistics on criminality and crime can remark that there is strong competition between themselves and other participants in terms of production, access, interpretation, and use. This is what Jean Marie Delarue mentioned, at the debate evening organized by the French statistics society, when he discussed "development of the right to competition" (Delarue 2006).

When we hear the term "public debate" we think of places where exchanges take place, with a comparison of ideas or interaction between individuals during which each one is encouraged to educate themselves, and give an opinion on information which is likely to have social, economic consequences, etc. Among these debate locations there are areas of the press, audio visual media, information sites online and more recently, blogs or even social network sites.

Statistical information made public does not necessarily become a debate subject. In order to be questioned in this manner, it must, at least, spark the interest of journalists so that they focus on it, and then transform it into a debate. We can therefore consider journalist as those who have a share of control in organizing public debate (Bardoel 1996).

A lack of comments does not always mean that a piece of statistical data is forgotten. Sometimes, one single report by a journalist can lead to significant media attention which places statistical information at the heart of numerous exchanges. However, a subject can be reported on a wide scale, without necessarily provoking veritable public debate. This happens when, for example, the article written is brief without comments.

Journalists thus play a role in regulating public debate by determining the degree to which they demonstrate statistical information which they receive from organisms "emitting/producing data" then they order the first sentence of the debate by choosing people they invite to take part in order to share their reactions. These guests may be political representatives, trade unions, association members, or experts in crime and in particular, in statistics.

When Gérard Mauger queries the participation of sociologists in public debate regarding insecurity, it thus accompanies his demonstration of reflection about the role of the media as "contributors to the construction of one of society's problems, imposing above all a wide repertoire of interpretation" (Mauger 2011).

Apart from journalists, we can share out those involved in public debate about figures on crime according to their position: as those emitting data, commenting on it, or prescribing it.

A producer of statistics on criminality and crime is only involved in public debate when he/she intervenes for one of these three purposes. Furthermore, including within the state, the producer of data is not always in charge of distributing it. Thus, the status of the organism producing the data is important as "all studies, all reports, all reviews, that is to say any type of document, can contain useable data, so long as the researcher can understand the conditions for data production." (Weil 2006). This does not only apply to individual researchers but also to all of those concerned by data.

If the model "producing/emitting" is the most common one in the administration, it may occur that the task of production and distribution of statistics can be attributed to distinctive organisms. This can relate to a case in which the service emitting data centralized statistical production of different entities.

Framework of distribution of official statistics: institutional communication or public statistics?

Statistics produced and distributed by the state can be described as "official" in that they constitute "an essential element of a system of information in democratic society, providing public administrations, the economic sector and the public with data relating to the economic, demographic, social and environmental situation" (UN 1992). In France, in the field of public statistics, the state played a central role in the production of statistics, since it is at the heart of it even, via INSEE in particular (Delarue 2006).

The fact that statistics are official is not just dependent on the conditions in which they are distributed, but also on the fact that this contest for official figures is one of the most significant sources of tension between political authorities and statisticians (Delarue

2006). There are therefore several statuses of official statistics according to which they are or are not inserted into public debate. Similarly, statistics which are considered "official" are not necessarily pieces of information which can be described as public statistics, that is to say which meet the criteria stated in the first article of the law no. 51-711 from the June 7, 1951 on the obligation, coordination, and secrets in the field of statistics.[2]

It is therefore possible that a public organization which produces statistics which does not call itself a public statistics body can distribute their information in a general framework that we will call "institutional communication", which means communicating information in a way that aims to promote the image of an organism of a government agency or at least to underline the efficiency of a particular political act.

In the field of crime statistics, the institutional communication includes all figures distributed by the ministry of the interior, the head of the national police or national gendarmerie or at a local level, by a regional police chief, or a national head of the police, or gendarmerie.

The production of official statistics linked to the activity of police and gendarme services relating to crime is ensured by the head of the national police including the head of public security, and the national gendarmerie. Statistics on non-road related crimes and offences are centralized and consolidated by the head of the criminal police.

This source of data is called the "état 4001" from the name of the form which existed, before the computerized format of this recording tool. It was used for the collection and transmission of statistics regarding incidents recorded, cases resolved, and people accused by police and gendarmes for non-road related crimes and offences (Padieu et al 2002 143-148).

The division of the head of the criminal police which has managed the état 4001 since its creation at the beginning of the 1970s, currently named "division of studies and forecasting",[3] is not and has never been involved in the system of public statistics and is even less of a "ministerial statistical service".

This expression relates to services of the government who train with INSEE, the public statistics service (the SSP) according to the article 1, paragraph 1, of the law from the June 7, 1951. In particular, it stipulates that "The public statistics service includes the national institute for statistics and economic studies and ministerial statistical services.".

It also defines "public statistics" as the grouping of "the overall information from all statistics produced" from, on the one hand "statistics studies for which the list is ordered each year from an order from the ministry responsible for the economy" and on the other hand by the "use, for general information purposes, data collected by administrations, public or private organizations responsible for a public service mission". It is also specified that "the design, production and distribution of public statistics are carried out in complete professional independence".

Furthermore, in between the public statistics service (SSP) and public statistics, "there is no exact coincidence" (Le Gléau 2009, 59). However, this lack of coincidence above all affects "some services producing public statistics", such as "The Bank of France or INED[4]" are not "part of the SSP, as they do not have the status of ministerial statistical services (SSM)".

---

[2] http://www.autorite-statistique-publique.fr/pdf/Textes_fondateurs/Loi_51_modifiee_LME_aout_2008.pdf
[3] Division of studies and forecasting.
[4] National Institute of Demographic Studies.

According to the rules listed, the use of purposes of general information of data collected by police and gendarmeries on incidents recorded relating to public statistics. Within the ministry of the interior, the division which manages them does not have the status of SSM.

This situation was discussed on the May 31, 2006, during a conference dedicated to the code of good practice in European statistics organized by the French statistics society, during an exchange between Benoit Riandey from INED, and Jean-Michel Charpin, who was then the general director of INSEE. His remarks were published in the fourth edition of the "Journal de la société française de statistique[5]" dated 2006[6]:

Benoît Riandey:
"You mentioned the ministerial statistics services. *What is most striking is that there is one ministry which does not abide by the 1951 law, given a lack of general statistics services. That is the ministry of the interior.* It is currently led by the former president of CNIS[7]",

Mr. Sarkozy:
"This would be the opportunity to create a ministerial statistical service which does not exist. Furthermore, three ministerial statistical services led by executives from INSEE were students within the head of the central administration. Paradoxically, the status of statistics has been removed from it, but its independence has potentially been weakened given that the head of the service for ministerial statistics was appointed to the board of ministers and no longer by the general director of INSEE."

Jean-Michel Charpin:
"In response to the first point made, I share your feelings, but I find your remarks a little harsh. Strategically, after having examined the situation of French public statistics, I said to myself: there remains only one ministerial statistical service; all the other fields are covered, and perhaps one day, we will need to group them all together, but in any case, no extension, apart from on one area, which is *that of statistics on crime and domestic security*".

There are two fields which are not completely integrated into public statistics: for one of these, this can be justified, but not for the other one. It is understandable with health statistics, which are only very partially integrated into public statistics. [.]. *Then there are domestic security statistics: political and historic reasons have led to this kind of information being left out of the field of public statistics, but this is not at all justified.*

Therefore, in strategic terms, I'm doing everything I can to encourage the re-integration of such statistics. I find your remarks a little harsh when you fail to discuss developments which have been very encouraging indeed.

The ONDRP is not yet a ministerial statistics service but it has, however become increasingly independent from the supervision of the ministry of the interior.

Nowadays, there is no more political interference in the publication of statistics and that is very significant progress. Secondly, the fact that the heads of ministerial statistics services are appointed to the Council of ministers is not something to be ignored: it is

---

[5] Journal of the French Statistics Society.
[6] http://smf4.emath.fr/Publications/JSFdS/147_4/html/
[7] The National Council For Statistical Information.

also the case for the general director of INSEE. Nobody denies this. However, it is important that the appointment to such positions is coherent with the necessary neutrality of those responsible for statistics (Charpin 2006, 18-19).

As we speak, the list of ministerial statistics services (SSM) was defined by the decree from the minister for economy and finance following suggestions from the general director of INSEE.

This process was modified during the revision of article 1 of the 1951 law on the August 4, 2008, which stipulated in particular which public statistics authority should be called upon for their opinion about draft decrees relating to the quality of ministerial statistics services. From now on, the list of ministerial statistics services is therefore established according to the authority of public statistics.

According to the former mode of appointment or the current system, the ministry of the interior never wanted the service producing statistics on non road related crimes and offences recorded by the police and gendarmes to become a "ministerial statistics service."

When Benoit Riandey stated, in May 2006 that "the ministry of the interior was not applying the 1951 law, one might presume that he means that these statistics should be entrusted to a ministerial statistics service."

It is in fact what Jean Michel Charpin replies to him.

As we speak, the list of ministerial statistics services (SSM) has been defined by the decreeof the ministry for economy and finances after suggestions from the general director of INSEE. This process was modified during revision of article 1 of the 1952 law from the August 4, 2008, which stipulates in particular that the authority of public statistics "is called upon for opinions on orders relating to the recognition of the quality of ministerial statistics services". Since then, the list of ministerial statistics services is therefore established according to the opinion of the public statistics authority.

According to the former mode of appointment or the current one, the ministry of the interior never wished for a service producing statistics in cases of non road-related crimes and incidents recorded by police and gendarmeries to become a "ministerial statistics services".

According to terminology suggested previously, the lack of willingness from the ministry of the interior to create an SSM on crime statistics means in particular that the service of the head of criminal police managing the état 4001 recording tool cannot claim that it represents public statistics.

As a result, the distribution of statistics on incidents of non road related crimes and offences by the ministry of the interior carried out in the past and is still carried out today only in the framework of institutional communication. This situation is at the heart of public debate on figures relating to crime.

Organization comparable to that of other ministries would have consisted, alongside institutional communication, of distribution for which those producing data would be a ministerial statistics service.

Reflection about the creation of a new organization for producing statistics on crime in public debate

For a public statistician, the initial organizational response to willingness to improve conditions of production and distribution of statistics on crime would have been the creation of ministerial statistics services at the ministry of the interior. Once this objective has been reached, one could have envisaged the creation of a structure which is the type for a supervisory body associating INSEE and ministerial statistics services and justice on the model, for example, of the observatoire national de la pauvreté de l'exclusion sociale.[8]

In the letter for the mission on the July 23, 2001, sent by the prime minister, Lionel Jospin to the members of parliaments Christophe Caresche and Robert Pandraud, they were asked to provide "work to define" a project for the clarification of "a new statistics tool" which "could lead to the implementation of a body to supervise crime".

The objectives to reach are described as the following: "It is a question of firstly using a statistical tool which takes into account real developments in crime, the activity of surveys and the follow up to data from legal institutions. [...] It would also be desirable to implement a tool that would allow, overall, to quantify the measure of the developments in feelings of insecurity. Finally, the government considers that conditions should be created for transparency in a subject as sensitive and close to the concerns of our co-citizens. This presumes that the ONDRP distributes in a periodic and regular manner, information on crime and responses which are brought by politicians involved in public security. This also presumes that the ONDRP ensures its mission in close liaison with the ministerial statistics services concerned.".

The measure of "developing feelings of insecurity" carried out by studies within households which within the public statistics system, is carried out by INSEE. Thus, it appears that services producing data capable of providing information for the ONDRP are mainly, the "statistics services" of the ministry of the interior and the ministry of justice on the one hand, and INSEE on the other hand.

The expression of "statistics services of ministries concerned" when it is a question of the ministry of the interior and justice under the name of the SSM Justice (the sub directorate of statistics and studies) which is part of public statistics services and the division of the head of the criminal police in charge of the état 4001 which doesn't belong to it.

The report of members of parliament Christophe Caresche and Robert Pandraud submitted to the prime minister in January 2002 and relating to the "creation of an organization supervising crime" does not however discuss this particular point (Caresche and Pandraud, 2002).

It notes that "the statistical tradition is an ancient one for the ministry for justice: the first publication of the administration of criminal justice dates back to 1825. Furthermore, this ministry has since 1973 had a veritable statistics service led by a statistician,", that is to say a ministerial statistics service.

The report never makes reference to the exact notion of "ministerial statistics services", and does not question the absence of SSM on crime within the ministry of the interior with a view to creating a supervisory body on crime. It envisages the eventual consequences of the creation of a supervisory body on crime on the services of the ministries in terms of means but not in terms of status: " [...] the dialogue with the supervisory body should necessarily lead to the reinforcement of technical teams of ministries by statisticians, [...] for the ministry of the interior, a reinforced statistical service should be created within the head of the criminal police".

In conclusion to the report, the members of parliament Christophe Caresche and Robert Pandraud wrote that "The creation of a supervisory body on crime is a necessity at the current stage of the debate on figures [...] In technical terms, there are many areas to be worked on: improvement; modernisation of the computer processing; progressive integration of overall statistics on crime; research of aggregates and relevant indicators; studies on series of phenomena which have not been explored in detail. [...] However, it

---

[8] The national body for supervision of poverty and social exclusion, http://www.onpes.gouv.fr/

is in terms of communication that the most innovation is needed. In fact, if the ministries retain their data and can continue to carry out publications, it is up to the ONDRP to carry out annual and periodical communication on crime figures.".

The report recommends the creation of a public organism having initiatives in terms of crime statistics which are extensive without envisaging the consequences in terms of coordination of public statistics and the lack of SSM on crime within the ministry of the interior.

The relations of the ONDRP with the courts of public statistics are tackled in a very general way: "It would carry out its mission in collaboration with organisms in charge of statistics at a national level, such as INSEE and in liaison with the CNIS (National council for statistics information created at the national institute of statistics and economic studies and in charge of coordinating statistical studies of public services [...]".

The role of producer of statistics which the national supervisory recommends in "annual and periodic communication on crime figures" is not explicitly associated with the notion of public statistics. However, in the absence of a ministerial statistics service on crime at the ministry of the interior, this leaves in suspense organizational questions that will need to be dealt with.

A new producer of official statistics which enters into competition with former institutional communication

The OND announced in January 2003. A year after the report of members of parliament Christophe Caresche and Robert Pandraud, created in November 2003 by the installation of its board of advisers. The decree which makes this creation official appeared in July 2004.[9]

Since its creation, and despite the weakness of lack of means given to it (just 4 positions), the ONDRP immediately committed itself to understanding and above all clarify the statistical tools which could exist in terms of crime and criminality. Above all, it leaned towards the état 4001 tool, tool for recording crimes, and offences by the police and national gendarmerie then carried out an assessment of other existing sources in private or public organisms before working with INSEE in designing a victimization study which had the vocation of being renewed each year.

In the past, during 2002, institutional communication from the ministry of the interior regarding incidents recorded by police and gendarmeries which became monthly.[10]

This new rhythm for publishing data fed public debate on figures relation to crime. It is therefore in this context that a "supervisory body on statistics which rises above suspicions" was created at the end of 2003 (AFP 2003).

While "in terms of security (protection of people and property) the collection of information regarding crime and the interpretation of quantitative data has always been an extremely sensitive historic issue, and in France perhaps more so than elsewhere." (Ocqueteau 2008), political authorities decided to implement a structure which would have to use and interpret data for which the ministry of the interior could no longer have complete control over its use.

The first OND publications were distributed at the end of 2004 in the form of different articles mainly to be used mainly for methodology[11] aiming in particular, as the main fundamentals of official UN statistics remind us, aiming to "facilitate correct

---

[9] http://www.legifrance.gouv.fr/affichTexte.do?cidTexte=JORFTEXT000000442860

[10] http://www.interieur.gouv.fr/sections/a_votre_service/statistiques/criminalite/2002

[11] http://www.inhesj.fr/?q=content/r%C3%A9sultats-et-m%C3%A9thodes

interpretation of data" by providing "according to scientific rules, information on sources, methods and procedures" used by "organization responsible for statistics" (The UN 1992).

As a result of the lack of revival and perhaps complexity in relation to a field which was previously tackled in a very simplistic way, these articles did not immediately benefit from access to public debate.

In January 2005, during a press conference, the ministry of the interior proceeded to its institutional communication on incidents recorded in 2004. It was then the only producer of official statistics on crime to intervene in public debate.

A few days later, in February 2005, the daily newspaper Liberation chose to "reveal" the results of one of the articles distributed a few weeks earlier by the OND relating to people accused by the police or gendarmeries of violence or threats.[12] This article, which escaped the attention of journalists, was therefore picked up on by a daily newspaper which dedicated its front page and a dossier to it.

This initial access to public debate from the OND as a producer of official data was made possible by an internal initiative of promotion of publications which went unnoticed at the end of December 2004 and also made possible by the interest of a daily newspaper in statistics relating to those under 18 accused of violence or threats.

We can also observe, in the way that the newspaper dealt with this article, tension between the emphatic title "Violence growing significantly amongst those aged under 18" and "Violence growing significantly amongst those aged under 18" and the editorial[13] which suggests taking "precautions" when interpreting the figures on this.

Another tension also exists in the original publication by the OND. There, it can be read that "The ONDRP considers that only one approach with the help of multiple statistics sources allows for the analysis of developments in crime and offences. This would be an initial approach and to carry this out, it relies on one single source; the état 4001 tool".

In both cases, clear objectives are simultaneously pursued, which can lead to a certain contradiction. According to Liberation, an attempt is being made to tone down a striking title on violence of those under 18 which is not necessarily part of the ideological tradition of a daily newspaper by an editorial which a lot less categorical. The OND is for its part, confronted with a dilemma. waiting to not be dependent on a single statistical source according to the methodology it recommends or publishes based on existing data by keeping the "multi source" approach for later.

Institutional communication of statistics extracted from the état 4001 every month[14] influenced the choice of the ONDRP. Before having published its first study, the OND was thus confronted with the existence of monthly distribution competing within official statistics.

Before becoming "a producer of statistics", the ONDRP carried out methodological work which is concluded by the definition of a general framework of analysis, for the particular case of the état 4001, and with a new working framework.

As Alain Desrosières, reminds us "statistics methodology" implies "a division of work between, on the one hand, 'experts' in the statistical tool as such, and on the other hand, the 'users' of it de, such as economists, sociologists, historians or psychologists" (Desrosières 2001).

---

[12] http://www.liberation.fr/evenement/0101518411-violence-des-mineurs-une-croissance-majeure

[13] http://www.liberation.fr/evenement/0101518407-precaution

[14] http://www.interieur.gouv.fr/sections/a_votre_service/statistiques/criminalite

The new methodological framework suggested by the OND was validated by its board of advisers at the end of 2004. The main characteristic of the working framework of the OND resides in particular in the replacement of the total incidents recorded also called "single figure", by a series of non cumulative indicators, which constitute "an initial concrete rationalisation of aggregates of transgression in criminalisation by a differentiated division of crimes and offences according to two major methods of reactive and proactive practices which were still never translated clearly in ministerial documents" (Ocqueteau 2012).

The publication, as of December 2004, of articles which only include statistics extracted from the état 4001 was considered by the OND as acceptable subject to insisting on the impossible nature of interpreting them in terms of crime committed and this, within the work carried out in particular by Merton (1957). This choice, which demands retention within the strict parameters of crime recorded and it allowed the OND to disclose its working framework. By offering different contents of institutional communication of the ministry of the interior regarding incidents recorded, it has become a producer of statistics entering into competition with the OND. Given that "the difficulty is not limited to gathering information, it also affected the meaning of information given" (Foucart 2001).

Having had access to public debate, the OND which in 2010 became the ONDRP (RP being the French acronym meaning punishment responses) recommends methodology which is not compatible with the use and interpretation of institutional communication. Any reference based on statistics from the état 4001 to "general crime", to "the overall rate of resolving crime cases " and any interpretation relating to crimes committed which are in contradiction with methodological principles defined by the ONDRP.

If a ministerial statistics services relating to crime had existed in the ministry of the interior, the competition between the use and interpretation relating to institutional communication or public statistics would have existed within the ministry, without necessarily coming up in public debate.

With a lack of SSM and to respond to the mission which was attributed in terms of crime statistics, the OND decided to insert its action in the framework of public statistics, as Stefan Lollivier has already noted in 2008, when he remarked that "OND now has all the characteristics of a ministerial statistics services and could become so in the short term if its increasingly significant role in public statistics was confirmed" (Lollivier 2008).

And since 2004, in a project summarizing a future annual report of the ONDRP submitted to the board of advisers that it is specified that decisions for modification and validation of statistical work is necessarily based on "statistical considerations". This expression is often quoted in the code of good practice of European statistics adopted on the February 24th,[15] and in particular in its sixth principal:

"*Fairness and objectivity* – Statistical authorities have to produce and distribute European statistics with respect to scientific independence and in an objective, professional and transparent manner putting all users at the same level.

Indicators

– Statistics are established on an objective basis determined by *statistical considerations*

–The choice of sources and technical statistics is made according to *statistical considerations*

---

[15] http://www.autorite-statistique-publique.fr/pdf/missions/Code_bonnes_pratiques_Europe.pdf

–Errors discovered in statistics which have already been published and corrected according to strict deadlines and those using them are informed of this.

– Information relating to methods and procedures monitored by statistical authorities are made available to the general public.

– The dates and time of the appearance of statistics are announced in advance

– All users have access to statistics publications at the same time and in the same conditions and all privileged access previous to the distribution attributed to the external user is limited, checked and then made public. Should there be a leak of data; methods and distribution were adapted to ensure equality of data processing.

–Announcements and declarations regarding statistics in the framework of press conferences are objective and neutral"

Claiming themselves as representatives of public statistics without necessarily being an SSM within the ministry of the interior, the OND "became independent from the supervision of the ministry of the interior" and publishes statistics relating to incidents recorded without "political interference" (Charpin 2006, 19).

The co-existence in official statistics in incidents recorded of institutional communication of the ministry of the interior and the distribution of "public statistics" from the ONDRP now has significant consequences on public debate on figures relating to crime.

It could be a source of confusion when two producers of statistics express themselves on the same day and sometime in the same place as was the case during the press conference on annual figures relating to crime which takes place around mid January.

Thus, elements from the speech of the ministry of the interior relating to a single figure on general crime or the rate of resolving crime cases and these are two elements missing from ONDRP publications whether quoted in public debate as emanating from public statistics by the ONDRP.

For more attentive journalists and in particular for those in the press or online (or even both of them for the newspaper Libération[16]), concentrated on the mission of checking figures used in public debate, publications from the ONDRP which allows them to put communications from the ministry of the interior into perspective or any people involved in politics which makes use of statistics on incidents recorded to in an incorrect way in terms of public statistics.

According to the way in which we access public debate, via the intermediary of a brief article in which the figures on crime recorded are associated with the ONDRP without referring back to adequate terms or based on a base article for which the journalist took note of the contents of the publication of the ONDRP and uses it in order to illustrate what in institutional communication is in contradiction with its methodology in a similar way to the ONDRP which will be very different.

Transition to the publication of monthly figures on incidents recorded in institutional communication towards a new organization producing data

Competition between those producing official data was at its most intense in 2005 when a monthly publication in the form of announcements on figures relating to incidents recorded from the ministry of the interior[17] co-existed alongside OND publications offering a working framework including figures relating to "monthly figures recorded by police and gendarme services" from an article published in December 2004.[18]

---

[16] http://desintox.blogs.liberation.fr/

[17] http://www.interieur.gouv.fr/sections/a_votre_service/statistiques/criminalite/2005

[18] http://www.inhesj.fr/fichiers/ondrp/resultats_et_methodes/lettreond3.pdf

In their board of advisers the general director of the national police, Michel Gaudin had reacted several times to OND articles on the use of statistics of incidents recorded by asking when the ONDRP would stop just using the état 4001 and taking interest in other sources as well.

A range of circumstances was necessary so that the most intense phase of competition within official statistics terminates with a compromise on conditions of publication of figures on crime recorded and "leads to a change in previous traditional communication methods" (Ocqueteau 2012).

In May 2005, we can read in a monthly announcement[19] from the ministry of the interior "A significant improvement in security since May 2002: with -10, 83% of crimes and offences recorded and crime in public decreasing sharply by -24, and 09%.

An increase of 6,42 % in crimes and offences recorded in May 2005 in comparison to May 2004, despite a clear increase in the activity of security services (+14,16% of offences revealed by the action of security services, +9,78% cases of custody +7,61% perpetrators accused as well as a rate of resolution of crime cases of 31,66%). Even a slight presence in prevention of crime by the police in urban areas due to the management of several street demonstrations which led to significant mobilisation of police presence. These police forces are usually hired for security purposes."

The lack of statistical neutrality can be seen in the terminology selected "significant improvement", of methods (assimilation of the total incidents recorded to a measure of security) and it can also be seen in the choice in the first paragraph, to have a period of a different kind of comparison of previous report where it is a question of the same month of the previous year. This was stated in the example of the first sentence of the announcement relating to March 2005.[20]: "The decrease in cases of crime recorded in 2004 is followed in March 2005 by -4,12% decrease in crimes and offences recorded" or cases in April 2005 "The decrease of the crime recorded in 2004 followed by April 2005 with a decrease of -3,13% of crimes and offences recorded".

The originality of the first paragraph of the monthly announcement relating to May 2005 can be explained by the willingness to avoid having to say at the beginning incidents recorded have increased by 6.4% compared with the same month of the previous year. As soon as this variation is quoted, it is followed by a series of statistics revealing "a significant increase in the activity of security services" which is presented as being in contradiction with the increase in incidents recorded ("despite").

Then in a sentence in which it appears there is something missing, the announcement offers an explanation of the increase in incidents recorded between May 2004 and 2005 which apparently is due to "even a little police presence as a measure of prevention in urban areas" caused by "street demonstrations or events which required the mobilization of police forces which are usually looking after different kinds of security".

This announcement from the ministry of the interior led to strong reactions from the OND as it had elements of interpretation of figures recorded in a very different way.

In December 2004, and in March 2005, the ONDRP wrote in an article and its first annual report (OND 2005a), that the collection of incidents recorded in may 2004 was incomplete due to a calendar including a weekend followed by a holiday day at the end of the month.

---

[19] http://www.interieur.gouv.fr/sections/a_la_une/toute_l_actualite/securite-interieure/archives-actualites/archives-securite/delinquance-mai-2005
[20] http://www.interieur.gouv.fr/sections/a_la_une/toute_l_actualite/securite-interieure/archives-actualites/archives-securite/delinquance-mars-2005

The first consequence of this was on the comparison of statistics in May 2004 with those from May 2003 as the announcement [1] from the ministry underlined at the time Crime in France (including the total number of cases of non-road-related crimes and offences recorded by police and gendarmeries) decreased by -10, 25% compared with May 2003.

One year later, when the completeness of the collection of incidents recorded in May 2005 had not been damaged; their numbers experienced a rise that the OND presented in its exchanges with the ministry of the interior as the inevitable consequence of the shortened month of May in 2004.

As of June 2005, the ministry knew that its institutional communication, and, later on, its process of collection of incidents recorded was going to be questioned in public debate by the OND as statistics are often called upon to prove the merits of government actions, or its failure according to its opponents (Mucchielli 2012).

This perspective seemed even more inevitable than the OND considering that the announcement had been written up in complete indifference to the work carried out and that it was without doubt going to try to defend its position newly acquired by the organization producing official statistics and trying to impose its opinions in the framework of a thorough and well argued initiative. And all of this in an initiative not intended for connivance or negotiation (Ocqueteau 2012) but to affirm its independence.

The reaction of the OND took place in September 2005 in a new article[21] dedicated to monthly statistics: it then took the decision to re-correct statistics regarding incidents recorded in May 2004 and in other months in 2004 for which it seemed to be relevant regarding the values observed.

The ONDRP then estimated that in 2004 "the months of January, May, July and October included 1 to 3 days of entering less data compared to the same months in 2003" and that the months of "March, June, August, November and December had a period of data entering which was longer in 2004 compared with 2003 (OND 2005b, 26.)" The ONDRP corrected monthly statistics according to the estimation of the number of days more or less of data collection.

By applying a statistical adjustment of data published without modification by the ministry of the interior, the OND pursued its initiative autonomous of the distribution of official statistics, which have been inaugurated by the creation of its non cumulative indicators.

The head of the national police also reacted in the same article observing that "the month of May 2004 was subject to a report for recording incidents recorded as that month was not concluded by a prolonged weekend of three holiday days. However, it is not possible to support the idea of systematic report as it would be contrary to the reality and to rules of recording data which were fixed. Furthermore, it is necessary to specify that the incidents are not deleted but reported for the following month. As a result, they are integrated into the total of the following month as well as in the total for the semester which is consolidated. " (OND 2005b, 25).

The disagreement over the generalization of the method for adjustment seems to be less of a crucial point in the relations between the OND and the head of the national police than the consensus which appears in public debate between two organizations producing official statistics for the month of May.

This means in particular that some affirmations from announcements by the ministry of the interior regarding May 2004 and May 2005 are in contradiction with the position expressed in September 2005 by the head of the national police itself.

---

[21] http://www.inhesj.fr/fichiers/ondrp/resultats_et_methodes/lettreond5.pdf

It is just one of the consequences of severe judgement within the ministry of the interior itself on these announcements. The main consequence was the decision taken from summer 2005 to transmit to the OND the responsibility of the distribution of monthly statistics regarding incidents recorded.

Thus, by applying methodology of public statistics in a field in which, with a lack of SSM, the ONDRP was absent and became a producer of official statistics which from 2005 was faced with strong competition from institutional communication on incidents recorded to the extent to which they modified the means of presentation and interpretation.

The compromise found within official statistics in order to avoid the most direct confrontation between two organizations producing data is above all specified in the introduction of the first monthly report of the OND dated February 2006[22]:

"In agreement with the ministry of the interior and the ministry for land development and given the work carried out by the ONDRP over the last two years, it is now up to the latter to publish and comment on the monthly developments in unlawful acts and criminal acts recorded by police and gendarme services.

The presentation of indicators of activity relating to police and gendarmerie services (cases resolved, periods in custody, those accused, records of prisoner arrivals and cases revealed by the action of security services) will be carried out by the ministry of the interior.

From now on, and according to methods adopted and validated by the board of advisers of the ONDRP, the development recorded by law enforcement services, measured based on provisional monthly data will be presented via three indicators: property crimes, deliberate physical violence and fraud and economic and financial violations. "

In practice, institutional communication of the ministry of the interior is not limited strictly to indicators of the activity of security services. Competition in the distribution of statistics on incidents recorded still exists but it is carried out in a well defined formal framework: the role of the main producer of statistics on incidents recorded by the ONDRP has even become and element of institutional communication nowadays.

In 2005, for the ONDRP, the distribution of a monthly report on crime recorded does not seem to be a priority of its project of developing public statistics in the field of crime. However, based on a methodological framework defined by the OND and perceived within the ministry of the interior as more thorough than that of institutional communication, the creation of a monthly report was an opportunity to organize competition more efficiently between official statistics, offering the ONDRP the possibility to distribute each month its own statistics methodology.

It is likely that in view of this process that the general director of INSEE describes in May 2006 "developments […] which are very encouraging" relating to crime statistics. Since 2007, the context in which the OND emits statistics on crime develops thanks to annual studies such as "Cadre de vie et sécurité" by INSEE-and the ONDRP.

Among all of these consequences linked to the role of the organization emitting official statistics on victimization by the ONDRP, this document will now concentrate more specifically on the way in which its action was received and commented on in public debate by the team of researchers which had in 1986 led to the first national victimization study in France (Zauberman and Robert 1995).

---

[22] http://www.inhesj.fr/fichiers/archives/ond-bulletinmensuel-fv06.pdf

Concepts introduced by the current article could be used in other ways which will perhaps be explored later. In coherence with the previous example, we once again tackle the question of competition encountered by producers of statistics a new arrival claiming that it is representative of public statistics such as the ONDRP in public debate on crime but this time relating to victimization studies.

Victimization studies: nature of competition between those producing official statistics and the team of researchers of the CNRS [23], a pioneer in this field in France

Jan Van Dijk, a Dutch criminoligist, reminds us that "from a historical point of view, national victimization studies were launched in the United States in 1972 in order to inform people more about political debates taking place regarding criminality and violence". However, he adds that "in Europe, the first victimization studies were carried out not by statisticians but by criminologists working either in research institutes financed by the government, as is the case in Holland, the United Kindgom, in Poland or in France […]" (Van Dijk 2008).

For France, the sociologists Philippe Robert and Renée Zauberman from the centre of sociological research on law and institutions dealing with criminal issues (the CESDIP) have been at the heart of the first national victimization study.

The CESDIP presents itself as the following on its website[24] : "The CESDIP is a mixed research unit from the CNRS (UMR[25] 8183), created by the n° 83-926 decree from the 20th October 1983. The CESDIP has a long history dating back 40 years, since it comes from the service for studies into crime related issues and criminology studies of the ministry for justice (the SEPC established in 1969. Since 2006, the CESDIP is a UMR with three supervisory bodies: the CNRS, the ministry for justice and the University of Versailles-Saint Quentin."

Again on the CESDIP site, on the November 14, 2008, an announcement [26] specifies regarding victimization studies that "Initiated at the CESDIP in the middle of the 1980s on a national scale, these studies were first of all perfected and made routine at a local level (regional plan in partnership with the AURIF[27] and a municipal plan in partnership with the French Forum for Urban security). After that, the CESDIP participated in the organisation of a national annual study by INSEE and now looks after the operations and systematic serialisation of it. The team of researchers which carry out these operations is composed of Emmanuel Didier, Philippe Robert, Renée Zauberman, Sophie Névanen et Lisa Miceli".

The CESDIP is therefore an organization for producing statistics on crime participating in public debate via publications and in particular those on victimization studies. It does not distribute what we call here "official statistics" as its works do not involve any public administration and in particular, not the ministry of justice, one of its three supervisory bodies.

In 2003, during the creation of the OND one of its main missions, the development of victimization studies, created a new situation for the CESDIP team having invested in this field for several decades.

---

[23] National Centre for Scientific Research.

[24] http://www.cesdip.fr/spip.php?rubrique1

[25] Mixed research unit.

[26] http://www.cesdip.fr/spip.php?article2

[27] AURIF is the Association for users of computing networks in the Île de France region.

The ONDRP associated itself with INSEE to design an initiative of national victimization studies according to the mission which was attributed to it in the recommendations from the Caresche-Pandraud (2002, 39) parliamentarian report which Frédéric Ocqueteau also calls "the most significant sales argument for the know how of the logistics unit of the OND" (Ocqueteau 2012). The fruit of the collaboration between statisticians from INSEE and those from the OND, as decision makers and consultation of a guidance committee made up of researchers such as Philippe Robert, terminated with the launch in 2007 of the first "Cadre de vie et sécurité" study.

This study, for which the collection takes place every year since 2007, from January to April, allowing the ONDRP to introduce itself as a producer of official statistics on crime offering a multisource approach (administrative data and data from studies) and multiangle approach (victimization suffered, feeling of insecurity, or observation of crime phenomena). It has also allowed for France to be put at the same level as other developed industrial nations in this field (Ocqueteau 2012).

The choice of the date of the publication of the annual report of the OND has, since 2007, been determined by the calendar of the study "Cadre de vie et sécurité": its initial results being available as of autumn, the ONDRP set the end of November the date of the appearance of its report.

It is in this way that in 2010, the ONDRP published its annual report on the November 23 with, as its main contents, the first results of the fourth "Cadre de vie et sécurité" study. The next day, the centre for sociological research on law and institutions relating to criminal issues (the CESDIP) released an announcement [28] online on national victimization studies. Firstly, it says "The ONDRP has just distributed summary results of the annual victimisation study cadre de vie et sécurité (CVS) carried out by INSEE at the start of 2010

Regarding these figures, the scientific world cannot say anything for the moment: the official ONDRP organises a ban which ensures that INSEE can only communicate data from the 2010 study to the research centre only in 2011. Only access to data will allow their thoroughly scientific analysis."

After that, the CESDIP reminds us that in the middle of the 1980s, with funding from the ministry for justice, the first national victimization study."

The team of researchers from the CNRS having led the first victimization study "in the middle of the 1980s" therefore intervened in public debate on figures relating to crime the day following the publication of the 2010 annual report in order to affirm in an announcement that the only condition for "truly scientific analysis" the results from the "Cadre de vie et sécurité" study made available to research centres including the CESDIP.

We can consider that these arguments express, in particular, the point of view of Philippe Robert and Renee Zauberman, since they refer back to it in an article dated January 31, 2012, on the daily newspaper website le Monde They declare on it that the measure of crime will not become credible unless a panel of real scientists, socialists in measuring crime internationally recognized by their peers in charge of establishing the state of crime by comparing all measures and observing their developments over a duration of time".

They refer back to the arguments widely developed in an article which appeared in March 2009 and telling many details of their own vision of construction of the national victimization study that they consider as moving away from their area of expertise and that they consider in particular as "the fruit of interests in common with INSEE

---

[28] http://www.cesdip.fr/spip.php?article534

researchers and the ministry of the interior which with the OND, has gained an intermediary for its questions. " (Didier, Névamen, Robert, and Zauberman, 2009). We will find this type of argument as saying in a concealed way that the study would have been designed by the ministry of the interior thanks to "an agency of the ministry of the interior" (Miceli, Névamen, Robert, and Zauberman 2009).

We can suggest an interpretation of these participants in public debate on crime statistics as a reaction of the CESDIP to what they perceive as competition in the field of victimization studies.

The competition of the ONDRP is presented implicitly as unfair since "the official ONDRP organizes a ban so that INSEE can only communicate data from the 2010 study to the research centres only in 2011. ".

To take value away from this competition, the CESDIP positions itself on a field of "scientific" legitimacy. This argument is underlined by expressions such as "truly scientific" (2010) and " (real) scientists) " 2012.

As Frederic Ocqueteau remarks, "this warning regarding the work of the ONDRP is characteristic of a completely Franco French tendency to believe that critical interpretation of quantified data on criminal phenomena should only be up to 'scientists' as if an impossible barrier opposed them to other interpretations which are less legitimate. This belief is founded on the need for putting a distance between other kinds of experts and scientists. In particular, given that renowned for being less forced epistemologically and a lot more listened to by politicians and the media. There was then a lot of tension between the different representatives of different kinds of expertise with their beliefs which seem sometimes to be a kind of a lecture to others" (Ocqueteau 2012).

Sent back in this way by the CESDIP outwith the "scientific world", publications from the ONDRP on victimization are qualified as "summarising" and their credibility is strongly contested. Competition felt by the CESDIP is of a very different nature from that of the first cases studied.

In fact, between the ONDRP and the ministry of the interior, the competition taking place within official statistics between an initiative which claims it represents public statistics and institutional communication. The feeling of competition regarding the production of statistics collected by agents from the ministry of the interior was moreover mutual. After that when the "official" producers of statistics entered into competition in public debate, the cacophony involved was subject to regulation within the administration.

The ONDRP cannot consider in relation to victimization studies, the CESDIP as a competitor equivalent to what the ministry of the interior can be in terms of statistics on crime recorded. For this, it is necessary for the CESDIP to produce official statistics where, even better still, it wants to publish data recognized as coming from "public statistics. ".

The existence of those producing statistics which were not official, a condition of pluralism of the use of statistics in public debate, is not necessary for competing directly with a producer of official statistics in its specific role, especially if it claims it is representative of public statistics.

It must be reminded that those producing statistics trying to insert their action in public statistics is held, according to the code of practice for European statistics:

to rely on the "scientific principles and methods", and to publish studies "with respect for scientific independence" (principle 6) It is also invited "when it is possible to organise", the co-operation with the scientific community [...] in order to improve methodology, efficiency of methods used and encouraging the development of better tools. (indicator 7.7).

The CESDIP, producing statistics positioning themselves outwith official statistics, did not react in public debate regarding contents of productions from the ONDRP, what would have been allowed, in particular, for questioning their appropriateness for principles of the code of good practice of European statistics. It chose to discredit the ONDRP, in theory as it does not belong to the "scientific world" However, such criticism appears off subject regarding producers of official statistics aiming, not as a scientific label, but as "public statistics".

For every researcher, the most relevant means for expressing needs and eventually its grievances regarding public statistics consists of addressing the CNIS, the national council of statistical information. In doing so, it does not position itself in a situation of competition but as a user of statistics distributed by official producers.

Thus, on the June 15, 2011, before the commission "Public services and services to the public" of the CNIS [29], in a short speech, Philippe Robert provided comment which might appear as a first element of interpretation of the reaction of the CESDIP of what it perceived as competition in the field of victimization studies.

Philippe Robert criticized the ONDRP without specifically naming it, for having given in to the "temptation of constantly starting afresh, in order to have the satisfaction of showing that they are the experts. "

For the CESDIP, the date at which it is presented into public debate as the first national victimization study is a major issue as it determines the status and the eventual reputation of its team of researchers in this field.

The initiative of the annual victimization studies "Cadre de vie et sécurité" starting in 2007, this date seems to enter into competition in public debate with "the initial study in the middle of the 1980s" (Miceli, Névanen, Robert, and Zauberman 2009).

Forgetting to remind us that the CESDIP was a first in France in terms of victimization studies "to have the satisfaction of showing that they are the experts. " only exacerbates "tensions" with the ONDRP.

In its opinion, the CNIS a major part of public statistics demonstrates itself as being more positive regarding the study and the ONDRP in general: "the current tools for collection presenting technical weaknesses which limit the capacities of public powers to respond as precisely as possible to these different expectations (in terms of knowledge regarding criminality) despite important progress carried out since the creation of the ONDRP the positive collaboration which is involved between the head of police and gendarmeries and the ONDRO and significant support from the annual "Cadre de vie et sécurité" study."

The CESDIP would undoubtedly have been less sensitive to the attention brought to its study in the 1980s if the development of "Cadre de vie et sécurité" studies led by INSEE and the ONDRP had not provoked a feeling of removal of the pioneer team.

In a country like France, the design of an annual national victimization study. This was something which could only be imagined within the public statistics system. From then on, the researchers could not have a role in the process of development as important as statisticians from INSEE in charge of the project, with little experience on the subject of victimization.

The project was started by an external request to the ministerial statistics service of the national education board via a recommendation from the board of adviser of the ONDRP renewed several times and insisted upon by its president at the ministry. It could

---

[29]http://www.cnis.fr/files/content/sites/Cnis/files/Fichiers/commissions/services_publics_services_aux_publics/2011/compte_rendu/CR_2011_1re_COM_services_publics.PDF

only be started once the statisticians from the national education board were able to work on it. This movement of the ONDRP was a means of asking for time and in the end, it led to a certain amount of disengagement on the part of researchers.

For victimization studies in the school contexts, the ONDRP has been able to play the role of catalyst between statisticians from the SSM of the ministry for national education and the universe of research represented by Éric Debarbieux, university professor, member of the board of advisers of the ONDRP, and sociologist Cécile Carra.

In this critical phase, during the design of the "Cadre de vie et sécurité" study in 2005, Philippe Robert chose as an emblem to contest the legitimacy of the OND, a position that he regularly renewed during each of its interventions or publications whether it be in a direct way or more often indirect way to neglect to mention the OND as being at the origin of ideas associated with INSEE in the implementation of the "Cadre de vie et sécurité" study whether it be carrying out work and statistics studies carried out based on the use of results of PCV [30] studies or "Cadre de vie et sécurité" studies.

In the announcement in November 2010 from the CESDIP we see the sentence "it is in fact at this stage (in 2007) that the ministry of the interior obtained from INSEE the launch of studies such as 'Cadre de vie et sécurité'" CVS studies. This is inspired by elements of rhetoric developed regularly regarding by the OND by its detractors and that it suggests that all requests coming from the OND have come from ministry of the interior which necessarily should discredit it.

Maintaining constructive participation during the process of designing a public statistics study can, of course, involve compromises from researchers, or even giving up on usual practice. However, removal or conflicts are choices which are less fruitful above all if one is led in order to use the study.

The conflict in which it was launched in 2005 Philippe Robert during the design of the "Cadre de vie et sécurité" study appeared seven years later as one of the main determining factors of the means of participation of the CESDIP in public debate relating to figures on crime. It explains, in particular, the willingness displayed by the CESDIP to compete with the ONDRP on victimization in public debate. While this position is not coherent with the status of two organizations between which on the contrary important synergies exist.

References

AFP Fil Général. 2003. Délinquance: un observatoire pour des statistiques "au-dessus" des soupçons, 04/11/03 12:26. ([31]Title translation: Crime: a supervisory body which rises above all suspicions).

Aubusson de Cavarlay B., N. Lalam, R. Padieu, and P. Zamora 2002. Les statistiques de la délinquance, France Portrait Social 2002–2003, INSEE,141-158. (Title translation: Crime statistics).

Bardoel J. 1996–09. "Beyond Journalism: A Profession between Information Society and Civil Society." *European Journal of Communication (London)* 11 (3): 283-302.

Caresche C., and R. Pandraud. 2002. Sur la création d'un Observatoire de la délinquance, La Documentation française. (Title translation: Creating a supervisory body on crime).

Charpin J.M. 2006. "Le code de bonnes pratiques de la statistique européenne: Genèse, élaboration et application." *Journal de la Société Française de Statistique*

---

[30] **PSV:** Permanent studies relating to living conditions.

[31] Title translation: summary titles of the book titles in French.

(SFdS), 147 (4): 7-28. (Codes of Good Practice in European Statistics: Development and Application. *Journal of the French Statistics society*).

Delarue J.-M.. 2006. L'indépendance de la statistique à l'égard du pouvoir politique. *Journal de la Société Française de Statistique*, tome 147 (4) (The Independence of Statistics in Political Power).

Desrosières A. 2011. Entre réalisme métrologique et conventions d'équivalence: les ambigüités de la sociologie quantitative, Genèses 43, juin 2011 : 112. (Title translation: Between Metrological Realism and Conventions of Equivalence.)

Didier E., S. Névanen, P. Robert, and R. Zauberman. 2009. La solidité des institutions. Les statistiques de"victimation" de l'INSEE (1996-2006), Genèses 2009/1, (174): 128-144 (Title translation: The Solidity of Institutions. Victimisation Statistics from INSEE.)

Foucart T., 2001. "L'interprétation des résultats statistiques." Mathématiques et Sciences Humaines (153): 21-28. (Title translation: The Interpretation of Statistics Results).

Le Gléau, J.P. 2009. "Les trois institutions de la statistique publique en France." Courrier des statistiques (126): 59-62. (Title translation : The Three Public Statistics Institutions in France).

Lollivier, S. 2008. L'utilisation des statistiques à l'OND. Un bilan flatteur, mais des pistes de progrès encore nombreuses, Rapport annuel, INHESJ/OND, CNRS, p.635. (Title translation: The Use of Statistics at the OND, A Flattering Assessment but with Ideas of Progress to be Made).

Mauger, G. 2011. La participation des sociologues au débat public sur l'insécurité, Politique, culture, société, (14), May–August 2011. (Title translation: The Participation of Sociologists in Public Debate on Insecurity, Politics, Culture society).

Merton R. 1957. *Social Theory and Social Structure*, revised (Glencoe, The Free Press), 147.

Miceli, L., S. Névanen, P. Robert, and R. Zauberman. 2009. "De l'instantané au long métrage. L'enquête Cadre de Vie et Sécurité dans la série des données sur la victimation." Economie & Statistique 426: 3-28. (Title translation: From Instantaneous to Long Term. The Cadre de Vie et Sécurité Study in Series of Data on Victimisation, Economy and Statistics.

Mouhanna C. and J.-H. Mattely, 2008.   L'OND : réussite politique et limites scientifiques, indépassables?, OND, Rapport annuel, November 2008, 623-635 (Title translation: The OND: Political Success and Scientific Limits which Cannot be Surpassed?).

Mouhanna, C. and J.H. Mattely, 2007. Police, des chiffres et des doutes. Regard critique sur les statistiques de la délinquance, Michalon. (Title translation: Critical Views on Crime Statistics).

Mucchielli, L. 2012. Les techniques et les enjeux de la mesure de la délinquance, Alterindicateurs, p. 93. (Title translation: Techniques and Issues for Measuring Crime).

Ocqueteau, F. 2008,   Quand un observatoire cherche à imposer plus de transparence... Réflexion bilan sur l'action de l'OND, Rapport annuel, INHESJ/OND, CNRS, p. 653. (Title translation: When a Supervisory Body Tries to Impose more Transparency... Assessment of the Action of the OND, Annual report.

Ocqueteau, F. 2012, "Une machine à retraiter les outils de mesure du crime et de l'insécurité: l'Observatoire national de la délinquance." Droit et Société 81: 447-471 (Title translation: A Machine for Dealing with Tools for Measuring Crime and Insecurity. The national Supervisory Body on Crime).

ONU, 1992, Principes fondamentaux de la statistique officielle, résolution C (47), Commission économique pour l'Europe. (Title translation: The Fundamental Principles of Official Statistics, Resolution C (47) The Economic Commission for Europe).

Van Dijk, J. 2008. Confrontation des données d'enquêtes sur la criminalité en population générale avec les statistiques de police sur les délits enregistrés, Crimprev, 2008. (Title translation: Comparison of Data from Studies on Crime amongst the General Population with Police Statistics on Crime Recorded.

Weil, R. 2006. Les techniques du recueil et de traitement des données, Sociologie contemporaine, Vigot, 2006. (Title translation: Techniques for Gathering and Processing Data, Contemporary Sociology).

Zauberman, R. and P. Robert, 1995. Du côté des victimes, un autre regard sur la délinquance, l'Harmattan, Paris. (Title translation: For Victims, A Different View of Crime).

Also of importance

Aubusson de Cavarlay, B., 1998. "De la statistique criminelle apparente à la statistique judiciaire cachée." Déviance et société 22: 2 (Title translation: From Criminal Statistics Apparent in Concealed Judicial Statistics, Deviance and Society).

Ocqueteau, F. 2005. "Observer les délinquances. Où, comment et pourquoi ? Sur la genèse de l'Observatoire national de la délinquance," in Peurs sur la ville, vers un populisme punitif à la française, J. Ferret and C. Mouhanna (dir.), Paris: PUF, 188-210 (Title translation: Observing Crime. Where, How and Why? Views on the Development of the National Supervisory Body on Crime. Fear in Cities, Progress towards French Style Punitive Tendencies.

Ocqueteau, F., J. Frenais, and P. Varly, 2002. Ordonner le désordre, une contribution au débat sur les indicateurs du crime, Paris: La Documentation française. (Title translation: Putting Order into Disorder, A Contribution to Debate on Crime Indicators.)

Tournier, P.V. 2008. "Vers un observatoire national de la délinquance et des réponses pénales, in Alain Bauer (dir.), La criminalité en France. Rapport de l'Observatoire national de la délinquance 2008, Institut national des hautes études de sécurité (INHES), CNRS Editions, 665-672. (Title translation: Moving Towards a National Supervisory Body on Crime and Punishment) Criminality in France: Report by the National Supervisory Body on Crime by INHES.

Tournier, P.V. 2010. Vers une base de données criminologiques sous l'égide de l'ONDRP ? in Rapport 2010 de l'Observatoire national de la délinquance et des réponses pénales (ONDRP), Chapitre «Réponses -pénales», Editions du CNRS, November 2010, 415-423.

(Title translation: Moving towards a criminological database under the supervision of the ONDRP?)

Tournier, P.V. (ed.), 2012. L'Observatoire national de la délinquance et des réponses pénales (ONDRP), Bilan et perspectives, textes rédigés à la suite du débat du 7 février 2012, au Sénat, présidé par M. Jean-Pierre Sueur, Président de la Commission des Lois du Sénat, Publication de DES Maintenant en Europe, février 2012, 34 p. (Title translation: Assessment and Perspectives, Texts written up Following the Debate 7th February 2012 at the Senate Presided by M.Jean-Pierre Sueur, President of the Commission of Laws at the Senate. Publication of As of now in Europe).

About the Authors
Cyril Rizk serves as Attaché Principal at the National Institute of Statistics and Economic Studies (INSEE), and Head of Statistics at the National Observatory of Crime and Criminal Justice Responses (ONDRP).
Christophe Soullez is Chief of the ONDRP.

Psycho-Criminology of Sectarian Reality

Loïck M. Villerbu

Abstract:

Universities or research laboratories rarely know how to equip themselves to study sectarian reality and offer diagnostic criteria from a criminological perspective. This is why too often it is not recognized that the victims of sectarian affiliations may have been under an influence, nor are they seen as the victims they really are, and they may find that sentencing in the criminal courts goes against them.[1] This influence upon them was not in the form of manipulation whose passive objects they may be or may have been— but because they themselves believed that they could give themselves meaning by (unwittingly) trusting criminal groups, whose foundation (sometimes in total good faith) is the scam. The work presented here attempts to show the construction of this sectarian fraud[2] and the Criminogenesis that it informs. This is not an essay in psycho-pathology on the psychological excesses of belief, although such may well exist.

We only have a small amount of relevant work on what could have been the first fruitful moments of the creation of such and such a group's sectarianism, a sectarianism that assumes all the opportune faces of fiction, of medicine, of care, of education, or of finance. Everything that calls itself and is named sect is not necessarily sectarian: for our purposes, what is criminogenic and criminal is sectarian.

A Framework of References

Speaking of a sect quite often leads to contrasting it with a church; the former then makes the latter out to be a sect that has succeeded in imposing itself to the point that the marginal dissidence that it might have constituted disappears in the name of assumed excellence. It is in a context of positive discrimination that equivalencies have been insisted upon and are often referred to as *New Religious Movements*. The problem is reduced to the problem of belief: each person has the right to believe what he wants. Studying sectarian reality from a criminological point of view does not mean studying a fact of belief but the concrete and criminal practices to which belief and its organization give rise.

The criminological context means that we are not fooled by the mere reference to beliefs, but consider from the outset what they elicit, impose, or solicit on the part of the adherent and social group.

Psychic disorder or social disorder is the pivot points of belief, not in what they are but in what they require as practices, conduct, and behaviors.

---

[1] In this sense, it is a matter of a phenomenon similar to the one potentially suffered by victims of sexual assault (sexual, psychological, moral) harassment, or conjugal violence. The denial of the earliest victims' speech had created mythomania (E. Dupré, *La mythomanie, étude psychologique et médico légale du mensonge et de la fabulation morbides* (Paris: Imprimerie J. Gainche, 1905), just as today, parental alienation syndrome runs the excessive risk of suggesting that the child is first of all manipulated by one of the parents and through resilience escapes by relying on his/her own resources.

[2] This is the follow-up to an initial work published in 2000. L.-M. Villerbu, C. Graziani, *Les dangers du lien sectaire* (Paris: PUF, 2000).

In other words, it is not belief as a body of knowledge that criminology will study, but the set of constraints in the name of which beliefs spread in coercive apparatuses under the cover of assumptions that encase the subject in a closed and terrorist system (life or death, life or the stock market), indifferent to law as well as to mental health.

The criminologist has nothing to say about the sect: it is a group fact, or religious sociology fact, a psychology-of-adherence-and-membership-fact, etc. It is its "sectarian" aspect that constitutes his object of study. By introducing a concrete project of belonging and not a study of a doctrinal corpus (whether written prophetically or not), the term essentially refers to practices of belief, practices linked to belief itself, and to its conditioning. These are the behaviors and their sources of inspiration (persons, milieux, ideologies, etc.) that will become the field[3] of criminological analysis. In other words, it is a matter of power-taking when one speaks of the sectarian,[4]–hence the possible semantic derivatives like sectarianism. Sectarianism bespeaks the uniqueness of a point of view, associated with the prohibition against speaking or doing differently. Sectarianism can therefore also be found in a minority group as well as in a majority group and it will take the empirical objects at its disposal: the *assumed or revealed knowledge* in churches or schools of thought,[5,6] *money* in groups that manufacture goods, mafia movements, the *forces* in apparatuses of control, relations to *sex* in socio-psychological apparatuses that yield liberation through the body, the *territories* in identitarian claims where borders are abolished, etc. In all cases, there is a single aim: wherever there is a plurality of opinion and individual practices, to conceive of only one formal, totally idealized type in complete accordance with the elements of dogma.

The criminologist is more than a specialist of criminal law since the question of deviance is his/her field as well. His domain is first and foremost the domain of the psychological sciences and the social sciences. What constitutes the criminologist's object of study is the set of operations through which, in a context of implicit or explicit intimidations, strategies are put in place and practiced that will progressively close off all possibilities for a person (or a group) to continue their self-determination and in so doing to lose themselves by taking another non-critical personality, for the sake of which the personality itself becomes invasive.

If the criminologist has a social role and a scientific goal, it is to produce a diagnosis of these strategies by deconstructing them into so many anti-personal and counter-productive stratagems on the margins of norms and rights. To analyze a sectarian action not only means analyzing dissident activities but also taking into account the ways that dissidence contributes to the destruction/self-destruction of persons, goods, and collectivity.

Criminological analysis centered on sectarian strategies and their impact leads us to employ psycho-criminology: the study of enforcement practices. It will be said that these practices are developed as a defensive process in situations that have become unbearable or risk becoming so. They are an outcome and an imprisonment in another mental and social status, on the basis of an imagined benefit (whose nature is connected to power,

---

[3] An illustration of this can be found via the philosophies that inspire penal codes on the one hand and, on the other, penal practices. Codes and practices are supported by philosophies, ideologies, ethics, and deontology, and their excesses are associated with what could be the disappearance of a third, critical term recalling the relativity of any corpus and membership.

[4] P. Denis, J. Schaeffer (eds), *Sectes* (Paris: Editions SARP, 1999).

[5] Chouvier, *Les fanatiques* (Paris: O. Jacob, 2009).

[6] J. MacDougall, *Eros aux mille et un visages* (Paris: Gallimard, 1996), 291-302.

control, and the means to obtain them). That is as much the case for the guru as it is for the follower, but of course in different ways. These strategies and their writing are to be envisioned on the basis of resistance to vulnerabilities that touch upon all the determining structures of social and mental life.

Sectarian reality is here essentially considered in its criminogenic dimension. The practices of belief (*rituals and doctrines)* are said to be abused and abusive, that is to say: recuperated by dominating pressure that is assumed a priori to be gratifying. These practices misuse *a single persecutory reference,* subtracting themselves from the imperatives of a society of law, with the enticing security *of a self-engendered charismatic referent.*

This allows the follower to be defined as a seeker of meaning, founding a demand for change on a single question serving as passionate certainty: the origins anticipate the construction of a future. The story is written, the goal is to recover it in order to profit or benefit from it. The price to pay is only one step in accessing this return (hence the frequency of propositions involving metempsychosis, "controlled" departure, billions of years of life, etc.). This seeker is active and not passive to the extent that he is on a quest—a quest wherein, he is told (as happens in other contexts[7]), nothing is obtained without effort and participation. What these efforts and participation requirements will be clearly stems from the founding personalities [of the sect] but it would be presumptuous to claim that everything results from these.

Sectarian Overtures

If we can therefore speak of sectarian intimidation as a placing-under-the-influence, this is only so due to a benefit expected in return. If there is indeed manipulation, it is in the context of a conviction to be re-established. This supposes that the deceptiveness of the overture, the so-called sectarian deception, be analyzed from two angles: first of all as an abuse of confidence, an invaded intimacy, an invasive presence. This deceit is practiced by way of a criminal manipulation of a fact inherent in the human condition, the need to make sense, *in a practice of believing in... or believing that....* Sectarian intimidation is an instrumentalization and a manipulation of customs associated with a need to believe, and with its mental economy. On this view, it has long been accepted that followers must have suffered from mental problems, from the most benign to the most dramatic or even that they believed themselves capable of unequivocally diagnosing acute periods (depression, separation, etc. that is to say, always a deficient state) and blinding themselves to the active factors causing a renewal of being.[8]

Next, the abuse of confidence coincides with an abuse of authority that in order to maintain itself must engender a policing of thought, an internalized and sometimes organized policing, as a condition of access and survival, of ways of being, suspending all initiative, alienating the subject to an unavoidable and persecutory rule. Dependence can only be established through cunning: one thing is taken for another (confusion of thoughts, suspension of critical states) and the means used will be those appropriate to achieve this. The deception is based on the objective while the means to render oneself credible must participate in the most accepted conventions or anti-conventions. Unknowingly (this part is a necessary condition), the follower then enters a process that

---

[7] It is the same process that is at play in various sorts of financial scams.

[8] G. Bronner, *La Pensée extrême: Comment des hommes ordinaires deviennent des fanatiques* (Paris: Denoël, 2009).

most closely resembles the Stockholm syndrome in a tyrannical and despotic group space whose roles are learned. Too often it is the initial victim state that has been emphasized instead of considering how this could be the result of a sectarian history (in a terminal form) that is closer to ruin—mental, financial, social, and somatic ruin.

What is written about the follower is easily found in what is written about the guru. Because, generally, we only identify this after the fact; we take a terminal state to be an initial one and endow the person of the guru with initial mental troubles ranging from neurosis to perversion or to various so-called personality problems. The problem is that anyone and everyone can suffer from such problems without contributing to the development of a sectarian group. Let us consider, on the other hand, that if there were severe mental problems at the start, we have trouble seeing how this could have emerged from the group since it requires a minimum capacity to be marketable. There are facilitating and opportune experiences but they can only be grasped as attempts to escape existential impasses that in and of themselves are not of a pathological nature. It is therefore necessary to produce the hypothesis that the one identified as such is the result of a sectarian group dynamic which is as much the product of the sectarian group as it is the producer of the sectarian group. That being the case, the question of escalation can be endlessly raised from either angle about the members of a sectarian organization. This escalation is not just formal; it engages each person in his own desires linked to the fact of having or not having power and exerting it.

Therefore, the guru is not always who we think it is; it is the situation of blindness we are in when we confuse penal responsibility and mental responsibility, psychological culpability, and juridical, ethical, and moral culpability, which leads us rather regularly to only perceive the faltering person as a monster or monstrous in his attempt to find a way out and build a separate world.

The guru will then be imagined as presence (whether charismatic or not); an invasive presence, in a logical and strategic way: "making himself father." This implies that ordinary and, up to now, learned relations might constantly be the object of a deconstruction. This group dynamic constructs specific power relations, ensuring the development of a one-way connection. It is surely there that we find those eternal sidekicks with multiple roles, leveraging and sacralizing the word of the guru: spokespersons and interpreters of decisions made and positions taken by the guru, whose gestures, postures, and stories need to stand midway between the true and the allegorical. Strategic sectarian rationality means *dividing* the adepts into so many tasks and routes to follow, *hierarchizing* them to guarantee ranks of subordination—the cement of every group—and in order to organize the *escalation* of which rivalry is the vector of a permanent overcoming. In fact, the other, the equal (the brother in the alliance) disappears and can only be hallucinated, idealized, whether in a positive or negative way; he is no longer someone!

The sectarian group is offered up and is imposed in relations of unending mirrors between guru (locus of all the power) and followers whose divergence from the norm comes to underline the salvific bitterness, a permanent narcissistic dissymmetry whose endless reflections will unendingly convey and elicit anguish from each person and the promise of days to come.

Leveraging his/her own presence	Hierarchizing the thresholds of proximity
Dividing up the followers	Forcing the escalation of merit and demerit

Table 1 : Logics of sectarian strategies

Sectarian reality is a reasoned construction, undermining the basic elements of social connection and mental life: it attacks the norms and constituents of social connection to realize a manipulation and a confiscation from it. Understanding this sectarian rationality will be easier when we better describe the different powers of societal regulations, and then the constitutive elements of social connection.

One objective here is to contribute to developing the diagnostics indices[9] of two experiential referents whose construction is progressive and sometimes simultaneous: the sectarian bond and then the sectarian undertaking.

The Sites of Sectarian Onset

1. The normative references of social regulation *versus* the deregulation of powers

All social life, by maintaining a capacity to live together, without being under an influence, acknowledges four foundational norms, each performing specific discriminations at their level of reality.[10] These normative pressures are the law, rules, habits, and ultimately customs. Referential constructs identify them in their difference: the code, the internal rule, habits, and the sacred. Like a grammar learned from spelling mistakes, these regulators are presented through deviation from them: the infraction is to the code what disobedience is to the internal rule: incivility toward decorum and disrespect toward the sacred. By giving rise to regulators, these organizing norms have singular operating modes: if the law is imposed, the internal rule can only be proposed; and whereas decorum is up for discussion, customs are invoked. The latter do not have a particular time because they are the origin of time. They justify their existence in eternity; they cannot be discussed insofar as they are the foundations of a world and its conception. These foundations are sometimes based on a book, and sometimes on an oral tradition; the book is revealed without intermediaries, and the tradition is legitimized by a potential mythology. Any explanation would be a tautology since this is about a world that is already there. Tradition, like the book, only assumes and leaves possible commentary that no historical or sociological datum can explain. Everything that is of the order of custom only assumes one mode of transmission, invocation. A social production follows: the fabrication of the believer and his/her corollary, his/her spiritual responsibility.

When it is a matter of Decorum whose customs are learned, through divergence from their foundation, in incivility, the modus operandi is immediately perceptible; if a custom is connected to a time, to a space, and to a given relational group, everything that is prescribed can only be discussed since it is resting on a consensual base. If the book or oral tradition are referents in customs, in decorum, then privileged books or types of cohabitation will be found that will be written in the form of etiquette, social habits, in the way to behave in such and such a situation. Given forms of proximity are constructed

---

[9] T. Lardeur and J.-P. Jougla, *Les sectes: Savoir les reconnaître, Comprendre leurs mécanismes, Les combattre efficacement, Aider les victimes* (Paris: Presses de la renaissance, 2004).

[10] L.-M. Villerbu et al. This is the follow-up to an investigation financed by the [French] Ministry of Education in 1994 on the topic of School Violence: etiology, clinical epidemiology, and its diagnosis [Violences Scolaires, étiologie, épidémiologie clinique et leur diagnostic] appearing in B. Charlot, J.C. Emin, *Violences à l'école: état des savoirs* (Paris: Colin, 1997).

amidst one's neighbors, and the objective is isolated: social solidarity in an exercise of moral responsibility.

Disobedience to internal rule refers to its organizing norm, the rule. For a rule to be internal, it is appropriate to see the emanation of it from a specific group that has organized a means of production in view of a transformable object. A group or an institution, an enterprise, constructs its performances on the basis of an agreement in a time that abides by the times of its production. It is in this context that the rule, in making itself institutional, offers a charter for a project facilitator from whom a certain form of excellence is expected. Moral responsibility and deontology are the unavoidable accessories of such a normative register. It is easy to conceive that contracts are created here, at least in an enterprise that each is free to leave or not, and thereby guarantees are demanded. Becoming a project actor has no other meaning.

Still, in contrast, the remarks that can be made about referring to the law presume many other statutes! By positing the infraction as the identification of a deviation from the norm, the law and to its writing, the code, the time constitute an obligatory reference here. It is also and correlatively the case for times, spaces, and territories. Times, because every code is modifiable according to the datable and referenced norms and values of an era. Law is not retroactive except to self-destruct to the extent that it has a commitment to the word and the promise of a broader community, in a time founded on alliance as well as its limits. In this way this temporality is quite different from the temporality perceived in the relation of Customs to the Sacred. In this sense the law is imposed and its codes are not up for discussion, except for their application in whatever concrete case. The commentaries of laws and their codes only have a distant proximity with exegetical commentaries. Here a law is imposed while elsewhere a custom is invoked: the object is no longer the same. In place of the spiritual responsibility of reference, the sacred, legal responsibility (penal, civil, etc.) is substituted, which is also different from the moral responsibilities attached to a project of production or to a form of vicinity or inter-vicinity. The citizen is born.

The sectarian propensity to co-opt the norm will attempt to reduce the set of organizing norms to only two, and for two different reasons. To make itself recognized externally as an autonomous identity, there will be demand for a particular status, benefiting from codes and internal dispositions, of an organization in a *defense of secrecy* system. The rule would act as a law: every project facilitator becomes a believer in perspectives. As for the second reason—in this case intended for followers—customs are claimed as the law *par excellence*; in place of the law's democratic foundation a text is substituted whose sacredness is not up for discussion. The law by its codes is necessarily metrical, the customs, by the sacred character of their references, engage an a priori intimacy with a transcendental deity whose only guarantor/guarantee is fidelity. And, along with it, an absolute loyalty to the group insists on moral responsibility grasped at the same time (hence the confusion) as spiritual responsibility. The law of the greatest number no longer counts; it would only evaluate the world from elsewhere to set (or set again) [the follower] willingly or by force on a road whose itinerary of truth is absolute.

Referents Organizing norms	Regulators Referential constructions	Gaps and definitions	Modi operandi	Axiological constructions	Axiological productions
Law	Code	Infraction	Imposed	Civic education	Citizen legal responsibility
Rule	Internal Regulation	Disobedience	Proposed	Charter	Project facilitator morale responsibility; excellence
Decorum	Customs	Incivility	Discussed	Etiquette	Neighbor Moral responsibility, solidarity
Customs	Sacred	Disrespect	Invoked	References to the book or oral tradition	Believer. Spiritual responsibility fidelity and loyalty

Table 2: Regulative structures of forces and alterity

2. Structural elements of social connection *versus* implosion of social connection: the two sectarian presumptions

Social connection is distinguished from a gregarious bond in the development of identitary constructs. The capacity to recognize oneself as existing (oneself like another and not confused with another) is connected to an entire history. This story borrows from nearby milieux or environments the norms and values through which each person will find himself different and similar. The implementation of a self is compounded with founding axes: gender and genealogy, inscription in a sexuated reference on the one hand, and the inscription in a reference of strata on the other. It is these two referents that are going to be the object of sectarian attacks.

Socio-ethnological, anthropological, or psycho-pathological observations account for the indices of a gendered construction. If there are only two anatomical sexes, there are three genders made apparent by psychological development or pathology, and by identitarian uncertainties. Individuation is preceded by a phase in which there is no self/other distinction and consequently no animate/inanimate distinction. A phase of omnipotence, animism, or transitivism gives rise to an initial differentiation, provided one is capable of doing so (autism, for example, displays some difficulties reaching this, and hallucinatory states display its regression).

A second accession is grafted onto this: the accession to sexual differences and to what that means in identificatory terms. Being a boy/being a girl and the bearable differences that means and implies. There, scientific literature identifies an operation that some do not manage to come through and denotes it with the term castration complex. Its impossible surmounting is the production of behaviors called fetishistic and an imagination or fantasies that all seek to deny the implacable reality raised to the status of truth. It is, as in the preceding phase, an ever-unstable acquisition.

What constitutes the third gender is not the gender of angels or hermaphrodites but the production of an irremediable exile in the approach to another reality. The masculine refers to norms other than the feminine. There are different modes of jouissance (and the sexuality invented there directly refers to it): men will now be excluded from the house of women and vice versa. To the point of discovering that it will never be possible to put oneself in the place of the other gender. That is an adolescent discovery, unstable as well as uncertain. The worst-case scenarios and the make-believe remain.

The sectarian presumption will unceasingly build its truth on a series of reifications: reification of a role in the state of nature or even circumventing an assumed role to denature it. Naturalization or denaturalization will be legitimated by the norm of sectarian self-engendering: the norm that assigns an ahistorical role to each position. Quite removed from affirming a natural difference between gender, or even status/role continuity, the sectarian attack in its ultimate idealism destroys the experience acquired by the division of animate/inanimate and transforms every Other into an entity obeying the law of original dogma. Hence the peculiar, enduring, affective disaffection that makes relations with convinced believers strange.

As far as relations of ascendance/descendence are concerned, the same scientific literature on kinship and parenthood orders constructs on three axes. The analyses deal with the verticality of an origin (time immemorial) or with the horizontality of belonging (in space with family boundaries). For the first we designate the genealogical fact whose principle is the principle of non-reversibility; no one can be his own father; there is no self-engendering. The traces of history are instituted in paradigmatic figurations whose totem (the claimed ancestor) is the guarantee, as an astrological sign might be elsewhere. The son makes the father by inscribing him as son of...

The second is double. It accounts for the generational relation; the one that identifies *the son or the daughter of...* This sort of generational construct is simultaneously learned in the prohibition of its confusion (the incest prohibition, its transgression, and the criteria of its transgression) and the recourse to the reference of minimum age of consent or alliance. It is discovered in the intra-fraternal by the recognition of a common inherited (nuclear family) or found (adoptive family) filiation. The only possible alliance and consummation of the latter (sexuality) is outside the family. The identified brother creates in rapid succession the half-brother and the non-brother, and partially opens the boundaries of familial spaces.

The sectarian presumption involving the complex relation of ascendance/descendence will consist of introducing genealogical forms that will be totally discretionary, only emerging from the possibilities of the Book or of oral Tradition and its upkeep. A story is always taken for the reality to come. The obligation to conform to this is assiduously policed, and deviations are always objects of punishment and repressive positions.

GENDER	Animate/inanimate	Boy/girl	Masculine/feminine
GENEALOGY	*Inter*generational	*Intra*generational	*Intra*fraternal

Table 3: the axes of construction of social connection on which
the sectarian presumption will be based.

3. The invention of a world in the throes of madness: Utopia, Ustratia, Uchronia.

From the Greek *eu* (well and good), an existential composition is sketched and affirmed in the order of time*s*, spaces, and relations. This composition is obtained through stratagems whose singular characters are worth describing.

- Reduction: Each person is no longer anything except a part of the One, the founder; every relation is asymmetrical and without recourse. Only the One knows.

- Every division is impossible to imagine and each instance of apartness is the figuration of a betrayal.

- There are as many relations as escalations to the extent that each member can only want more presence for self, more founder.

- Hierarchization. Powers give rise to ranks that are inherited/assumed and never confirmed once and for all. The ranks occupied come with the benefits of physical proximity with the One.

Thus for a world euphemized in self-engendered spaces, each person's differences are only real in a relation to the different powers created and whose function is maintaining an abstract of reality outside the time of the world. Enigma and therefore mysteries are at the foundation of these euphemizations and their upkeep through intimidation or endless partying. It is in this sense that the normative foundations of a sectarian influence can be identified.

The guru is not the one who is the most visible.

This will to proceed to the analysis of the guru through the social productions that he has managed to realize is doubly ambiguous.

First of all because we only have the terminal states of it. Setting off from behavioral actuality to read personality traits there means denying a personality's history and naturalizing it. To say that the social production that a sectarian group consists of is the reflection of the psychological characteristics of its founder denies the effects of distortion that have been engendered, the modes of access, or the devices that have permitted the observation. Anything else is to determine the characteristics of a sectarian group, but to misconstrue the risks that have been taken. If it is possible to profile some of the ways that sectarian groups function, through the study of the effects of their normativity, it is impossible to predict something other than the elements of vulnerability that will be its own in the confrontation of opportune situations.

Next, it is illusory to consider the guru the master of the sectarian group; consequently he, too, is constructed by the group and the latter's demands. In this sense he himself must constantly strive toward overcoming for the upkeep of the founding enigma like constituted territories.

Can one then go back upstream from the characteristics of sectarian influence to the one that produces this influence? There is no doubt that one person comes to found a sectarian group on the basis of a personal problem to be resolved, in an ideological context of resistance to what constitutes authority. The sectarianizing group will be the vehicle for this: it must be admitted that this will also inflect dogma and its modes of application. The founding figure is then forced to strengthen an *avatar*, a charismatic personality taking its possibilities, sometimes extreme, to their limits. It is the relation to this screen or this avatar that performs the calculations and manipulations of the one who leads the sectarian group. That is to say, the moment when dissidence takes the lead in a fight *for life* with methods that will break all resistance—wherever this resistance may be, and with the extreme methods that that produces: by removing all humanity from the other, from the stranger. This is what legitimizes and justifies all the artifices and props of power.

Sectarian deception is not the fact of taking oneself (this would only be a mythomaniacal fable or delirium) to be someone but to make believe that the proposed solution is the best for everyone; that there will be life and survival for the greatest number of the elect. The deception is constructed with all the tricks proper to it and can be at best defined with two generic terms: deception and sacrifice. These methods of...will be deployed in two constructs: the sectarian bond, that is to say the progressive development of thought distortion and sectarian labor, the affirmation of belonging to a group apart.

Sectarian bond. It is a bond *without reciprocity*, for an expectation defined once and for all. The absence of reciprocity makes the absence of contribution, despite appearances (for example money, time, work, etc.): to give, there must be the possibility to consider the one whom we hold up as different from ourself; here, the other, the one who receives, is taken to be the container of every other. Consequently, it can only be a matter of a restitution. The proof would again lie in how there is no counter-offering in this group. The one who receives does not give in return; he promises what he will not be able to give. Granted, he can offer better times, but only as one advances a sum of money for subsequent reimbursement. In contrast, the debt is magnified in the ideality of a mutualization on the grounds that everything must contribute to the same progress. This mutualization is inscribed in a wider coercive project.

A fourfold intimidation control, always under cover of rituality, is exerted over existential parameters.[11]

Control of Bodies:

- Feeding is justified on the basis of an active cosmogony. What would constitute a diet and regimen as part of a medical prescription is given here as the fact of following or obeying a world order. Whether in ascesis (restriction) or consumption, there is the choice of some foods and the rejection of others, the composition of foods. Feeding cannot be done for pleasure but to attain (or nourish!) a superior state of consciousness, another lucidity; and the result is also the pursuit of least resistance.

- Sexuality, forbidden or reduced follows the same objectives. It cannot be a sexuality with a chosen partner; that would be deviation. It can only be participation in another order of the world: an energetic resource that becomes impoverished or is to be fed, a link between cosmological entities. Chastity and lewdness are brought together and required for the same reasons.

Every relation to the body is a dramatic corporality to the extent that it imposes the need to deal with it. On this basis, in taking power sectarian dogma can only enslave: it is the technique of the constrained body. Purification is punishment. The body and what comes from it can only be the object of control to the extent that it is always susceptible to speaking for itself, to having autonomous needs.

Control of Interpersonal Relations

To the extent that the sectarian group personifies its creator, all individuality is a vehicle for menace. What would be duality is deviationism. All outside relation is indicative of a plot to the extent that it can put in the balance attachments of fidelity or loyalty. Every relation is coded in its principle; the force of the rule of life is to constantly maintain the presence of an authority whose jouissance cannot be contested. Every relation is first of all a relation in a hierarchy of belongings. Distance and proximity with the founder are the object of a permanent vigilance and followers will sometimes self-identify with the rank or the stratum that they occupy. Let us also note the control over relations by means of fetishistic objects supposedly effective in rebuffing potential and/or supernatural invaders.[12]

---

[11] Works and articles containing adherent testimony display on this topic remarkable convergence in the variety of residential sectarian spaces. F. Roncaglia, *Mandarom, une victime témoigne.* (ed. TF1, Grands témoins, 1995). I. Sebagh, *L'adepte. Tous dans l'enfer d'une secte* (Geneva: Le comptoir des éditions, 1996). J. Miscavige Hill, L. Pulitzer, *Rescapée de la scientologie* (Kero 2013) [J. Miscavige Hill, Lisa Pulitzer, *Beyond Belief: My Secret Life Inside Scientology and My Harrowing Escape* (New York: Morrow, 2013)]. J.R. Lewis, *The Order of the Solar Temple: The Temple of Death* (Ashgate Publishing Limited, 2013).

[12] In the same sense, one will notice the ease with which certain sectarian movements appeal to the law and to rights in order to escape from the accusations levelled against them. Thus in Paris, 2005

Control of time.

Time is regulated according to the time of foundation and consequently requires the development of calendars. But, beyond this aspect, a proper temporal dynamic will see to its inscription in the time of another world order: prophetic times, messianic times, times of the end of the world; millenarianisms mix with the techniques of controlling awareness of time and duration. Natural cycles and apocalypses, times of return. So many temporalities that have their vulnerabilities and are risk factors. It is the search for opportune, precipitating (natural) moments, the cosmic catastrophe, or the conviction of a return elsewhere (suicides and celestial transportation of bodies), or the organization of (armed) resistance.

Control of spaces.

There are no sectarian groups without the creation of a totally private territory (fear of outside observation or of surveillance by third-parties) or one fashioned in the image of an invented world. The territory is a resistance to dispersion. This space is in its invention similar to created time: coded—not from a functional point of view, but organized as a demonstration of a higher power. The control of spaces or of modes of habitation is done according to plans: the map takes precedence over natural space. Sectarian geopolitics is constructed on an imaginary geography, the geography of the book and/or of tradition. From there, the search for inviolable, withdrawn, surrounded sites that sometimes rise into quasi-cathedrals and sometimes erase all visibility as far as possible. Invisible and active in resistance.

Sectarian Work: the Conversion

One can speak of the sectarian undertaking as one speaks of amorous work or of the work of mourning: a mental labor of recomposition. The emphasis placed on the word *work* indicates that it is about operating procedures, not aleatory at all, organizing itself around strategies for taking power. The implementation of the sectarian bond opened the way to this deeper work of *recomposition* (R-NTI): *negation* (of norms and existing values), *transgression* (affirmation of positive effects of this negation)–*inversion* (realization in ordinary life of the transgression that has a value in the realm of initiation and definitive belonging). The transgression is not only made possible, it becomes an obligation and the trace of belonging, like an indelible tattoo. It is done on the foundations of the social bond, hence its profoundly destructive effects.

- Work on the reference to genealogy. All material and immaterial heritage, like the exercising of parenthood is in itself a form of perversion, underpinned by incestuous relations. Patrimonial goods are "bad, doubtful" and to be set aside to liberate oneself from an original debt.

(AFP) "The Paris Court of First Instance [Le tribunal de grande instance (TGI)], ruled against a group of attorneys and several plaintiffs who wished to see the dissolution of Unadfi, specializing in information on sects, and sentenced them to pay damages, it was learned Wednesday at the TGI. An association of attorneys linked to the organization Cap for Freedom of Conscience ['Cap pour la liberté de conscience'] summoned the National Union of Associations of Family and Individual Defense to demand its dissolution, accusing it of being 'thought police.'"

In such a framework, woman is, more than man, the rival of the founder. She is *par excellence* the person who escapes control. She is necessarily in an ambivalent position, partner or mother, cloistered in a maternal role, or bound for covert prostitution. Idealized, she is unattainable except through and in a code specially invented and written in a Book. The same goes for the child, who is to be formatted (Angelization of the child or a priori perversion) or the man (whatever the attributed status) who could be an adversary; his being reduced to disciple or woman is part of the initiatory itinerary. Two solutions are possible: destruction of the familial bond as the conditions of access, or constraints to be imposed on the family (Moon's obsession with and fetishization of the couple, obsession with and fetishization of the group, or the partner-swapping in ISO ZEN or AAO, etc.). In every case, what is demanded is a (reifying) return to a fictive state of nature, invented for the needs of dogma. Status is less important than the functional role to be played in a mode of "time immemorial" that organizes its return.

- Work on gender. Genealogy was put in the service of dogma; the brother had disappeared, the confusion of generations replaced the prohibition on daughter–father, mother–son incest, and the daughter/mother like the father/son were forgetful of all kinship ties to become something "consumable": generational confusion. Gender in its three constructs (animate/inanimate, son/daughter, masculine/feminine) will regress to only one of them: a forcing of limits of the animate/inanimate relation symmetrical to the deification of the enterprise carried out by the guru.

On the one hand, this will be the negation of the ordinary limits of life and death. It will be realized in two ways: first, through a regulation of the principle of vital fluids, the regulation of exchanges of blood, of medication (forbidden infusions, prohibition on salt in food, medical inventions, imaginary and always secret pharmacopeias, etc.). Second, through proximity to dangerous animals, or situations of high-risk to life, etc.). Protection is guaranteed by proximity to "the first elect" or objects that belong or formerly belonged to the latter. *Predestination and proximity. Mother Nature.* In one and the same sense, the daily organization of work that allows no remuneration that might be understood as suggesting some sort of autonomy.

And on the other hand, self-mutilating behavior, debasing mutilations (for example, castration, various amputations) and, potentially, "transportation" by assisted suicide. Giving death does not mean taking life but offering a solution or even making the non-believer disappear, who, as such, is devoid of rights.

- What is the future of these sorts of constructs given the experience of the current situation?

Two responses are given by the study of sectarian groups that have been led to their total or partial ruin: death or a perpetual change in successive metamorphoses; the proliferation of a policing of mores and the attempt to regulate or judicialize rigidly all deviations from standards and gaps identified in a book or following an invoked tradition. That implies painting over everyday reality in order to avoid being the object of judicial actions (kidnapping, sequestration, etc.).

Sectarian work has constructed a closed world. This world keeps secret its ruin or the destruction of the outsider. Its peculiarities can be described with many diagnostic symptoms.

1- Enclosure and breaking away from the world of the non-elect or the common world. This enclosing is both internal and external. The external and internal boundaries are reinforced. The borders engender their own persecution. It the plot that prevails in the realm of relations. The outside is the locus of all the destruction to come.

- The overriding focus on the microbe in the internal realm: whether it is lurking in the food or explodes in suspicions of internal bad intentions. On the one hand, permanent suspicion of plots against legitimacy, a calling into question of the healthiness of non-prescribed relations where such things are so many self-productions of attempts to place oneself outside the common realm of men. On the other hand, hyperawareness of the degradation of the world: deaf hostility from all quarters and everything is disintegrating. This, in turn, is used as a means of repression: hygiene and cleanliness that are beyond obsessive with means that are hardly adequate.

2- Any search for autonomy is a sign of giving up and the latter is an indicator of a lack of faith. Informing is advocated as the supreme weapon, purification as a requisite to prevent the contamination of the human environment.

3- Unleashed utopia. The internal reinforcement of obligations requires fortifying what remains dynamic (hypostasized Energy). This reinforcement will take place in extreme behaviors of hypercontrol (in an ascetic, juridicist, or obsessive mode of planning) or permanent (orgiastic and ordalic) agitation.

4- The world is reduced to two dimensions, into dependency, hence a single language, hence social phobias. A critical dimension disappears and the figure of the other becomes projective: it is and becomes the non-acceptable in itself, is rendered apparent, petrified, in and by the other.

5-Ineluctable tribulations: we have seen vagrancy and the search for margins in *a high and dry* place. The truth is jealous, distrustfulness, suspicious, and always fears being stolen. A territory is elected as axis of the world and plays the role of "survival island", along with the possible provision of "survival kits." We know about the attempts to give oneself a sheltered space (a boat in non-territorial waters, or farther away, in inhabited spaces, in places that allow the permanent representation of the axis of the world,[13] everything that goes vertical and assures the link between the worlds up high and the worlds down below. It is known what attempts are going to fail, to find in the most hostile of jungles or in a bunkerized *space* a remission from the attacks that have been endured. Faith does not imply surrender; it is a game of life and death. Killing/suicide are alternatives with the same end. What appears to outside observation as a sacrifice is not one. It is a programmed rebirth.

The other version of the programmed end is rebirth in another form; where the sectarian group was able to give itself something to see in a straightforward way, this contributes to its dispersal and its dilution in screen space, the mailbox of its survival.

Prospects

Is there a real difference between sectarian groups and the groups defined today as "terrorists"?[14] Nothing is less sure. Granted, the conquest of territories (with the destructive and selective practices that that assumes) where faith can rest, a book, a tradition, in an invariable reading, does not take the same armed routes in most cases.

---

[13] T. Huguenin, *Le 54ᵉ* (Paris: Laffont, 1996 [2001]).

[14] With all the ambiguity borne by this term to the point that by extension one might have written that one could always be someone else's terrorist whenever terror was used; a moment and ultimate vector of recognition. But other studies have also been able to articulate the difference between resistance and terrorism on the basis of a different analysis of destructiveness. G. Rabinovitch *De la destructivité humaine* (Paris: PUF, 2009); E. Fromm, *La passion de détruite. Anatomie de la destructivité humaine.* (Paris: Laffont, 1996 [2001]) [*Anatomy of Human Destructiveness* (New York: Holt McDougal, 1973). M. Trévidic *Terroristes. Les 7 piliers de la déraison.* (Paris: J.C. Flattes, 2013). Karl Laemmermann, *Anders Behring Breivik: Terroriste norvégien d'extrême droite* (CreateSpace Independent Publishing Platform, 2012).

Events virtually all over the world linked to the reconquest of a territory in the name of a faith follow, however, all the same roads and errors.[15] The essential differences lie in the declination of objects (money, sex, corpus of knowledge, territory, faith, etc.), of powers and the removal of the latter. And the same goes for mafia groups: in these examples it is a single movement of dispersion, individualization, instability of assemblages that can be observed.

For lack of truly criminological perspectives, numerous studies remain in the closed and fragmented spaces of disciplinary learning or in offices, classified as defense secrets. The same goes—as indeed it does—congruently, for all those social objects that remain as orphaned knowledge because the means are lacking for them to be constructed into a totally separate, complex discipline that might synergize researchers and practitioners.

The challenge of this diagnostic knowledge is fundamental. From both the point of view of prevention and the creation of supportive units when the time comes for departure from these criminal groups, the support provided to departing members of criminogenic sects poses as many problems as someone leaving any criminality behind.[16] Without a network policy symmetrical with the deadly envelope of the preceding group, escapes remain gravely traumatic and unstable.

About the Author

Loïck M. Villerbu is a Professor Emeritus at Université Rennes 2 and Paris VII. He works in the Institute of Criminology and Humanities, Interdisciplinary Center for analysis of human and social processes. (*Institut de Criminologie et Sciences Humaines, Centre interdisciplinaire d'analyse des processus humains et sociaux*).

---

[15] M. Pignot, *L'enfant soldat, XIX—XXI siècle* (Paris: Colin, 2012). In particular, E. Medeiros "De la terreur à l'illumination," 139-159.

[16] P. Mbanzoulou *Insertion et désistance des personnes placées sous main de justice. Savoirs et pratiques.* (Paris: L'Harmattan, 2012).

Al Qaeda's Western Volunteer Corps

Mitchell D. Silber

As the hostage crisis and terrorist attack on the In Amenas Algerian gas complex unfolded over four days in early January of 2013, security and terrorist experts were quick to point to Al Qaeda in the Islamic Maghreb (AQIM), the North African Al Qaeda affiliate, as responsible for the heinous acts that resulted in the death of 38 Westerners. Flush with cash from years of kidnapping and ransoming Western hostages and well-armed after Qaddafi's substantial weapons depots opened up, many had said it was only a matter of time before AQIM raised their game and attempted more sensational attacks—which clearly the In Amenas attack represented.

However, what has surprised security and terrorist experts worldwide has been the confirmation that among the attackers, and potentially in leadership roles, were two Canadians in their 20s—both from middle class families from Ontario.[i]

In a related matter, when a British journalist and his Dutch colleague were kidnapped by an Al Qaeda related group, Al-Dawla al-Islamiya, in July of 2012 as they crossed into Syria from Turkey, some of their captors turned out to young men with distinctly "south London accents". These British born jihadists had noted that, "we're not Al Qaeda, but Al Qaeda is down the road," suggesting a loose affiliation. However, they were members of a group of foreign fighters battling against Syrian government forces and their group, which numbered between 30 and 100, had close to 15 British nationals in it.

In October, Shajul Islam, a 26-year-old British doctor who worked for the British National Health Service, was arrested upon his return from the Middle East to the UK at Heathrow airport for his alleged participation in this very kidnapping as well as other terror-related offences.[ii]

Similarly, in March of 2012, three attacks with a firearm occurred in the French cities of Montauben and Toulouse resulting in the death of seven people and the serious injury of five others. The perpetrator was a French citizen, 23-year-old Mohammed Merah, who had traveled at least once to Pakistan and Afghanistan, where he may have received some paramilitary training, but who radicalized to violence in Toulouse.[iii]

Though the events in Syria, Algeria and France are separated by hundreds of miles and the nature of conflict in each environ is quite different, the presence of young Western-born foreign fighters who were radicalized to violence in London, outside of Toronto, and in Toulouse underscores a important trend worthy of the attention of terrorism experts and security officials worldwide—almost a dozen years since the attacks of September 11, 2001, "Al Qaeda"[iv] is still able to call upon, both formally and informally, an international corps of Western volunteers to fill their ranks to join larger Islamist struggles abroad as well as at home and to indirectly continue to make war against the West and its allies. Radicalization in the West is unfortunately still alive and well, just manifesting itself in new ways in 2013.

The resilience of this phenomenon triggers a number of important questions. How significant is this threat from Westerns who radicalize to violence? What has its frequency been and how has it manifested itself over the past few years and what is its potential impact globally and locally in the West? As Western police, security and intelligence services struggle to detect and disrupt these homegrown terrorists, where is the balance between civil liberties and security?

Recent Trends Among Western Jihadists

Dating back to the international brigades of the Spanish Civil War in the 1930s to more recent campaigns in the Balkans and Africa, British, Canadian, American, and French citizens of varied ethnic and religious backgrounds have volunteered to take part in overseas military actions as mercenaries, freelancers, freedom fighters, or self-proclaimed holy warriors. Their motivations have run the gamut from ethnic, religious, or ideological zeal, to a desire for adventure or heroism, and often for both.

Since the attacks of September 2001, with increasing frequency, Western volunteers from London, Toronto, New York, and Paris have traveled to war zones in an effort to fight overseas, receive paramilitary training, develop skills, provide supplies for or to receive sanction and direction from Al Qaeda or one of their affiliates or allies. Some of these individual have returned to their home countries to launch devastating attacks like the London July 5, 2005, tube and bus bombings on behalf of Al Qaeda. However, others have chosen to volunteer to act at home, on Al Qaeda's behalf, without traveling overseas. Together these two groups represent Al Qaeda's Western volunteer corps.

This article will consider and discuss the most relevant events in France, the United States, the United Kingdom, and Canada since 2010 to provide a survey of some of the most recent manifestations of this phenomenon over the last three years in the West.

Canada

Since September 2001, the most significant plot against Canada had been the "Toronto 18" plot, which was disrupted during the summer of 2006. As many as 18 men, primarily with Canadian citizenship, but from diverse backgrounds, plotted to attack the Canadian Security and Intelligence Service building (CSIS), the Toronto Stock Exchange, and a military base near Toronto. Using informants, this plot was disrupted by Canadian authorities as the men were taking delivery of ammonium nitrate. Though the plot was not linked to Al Qaeda, the men were inspired by Al Qaeda. The most significant plots in Canada since 2010 include:

Project Smooth

In April of 2013, two individuals were arrested in Montreal and Toronto, who were alleged to be plotting to attack a train operated by Via Rail Canada, the government-owned rail system, that travels between Toronto and New York City. According to the Royal Canadian Mounted Police (RCMP), the two men had studied train movements and rail lines in and around Toronto.

The plot was to derail an Amtrak or Canadian Via train as it crossed over the Whirpool Rapids Bridge from Canada into the United States. The effects would have been devastating had they succeeded, as a 115-year-old arch bridge spans the Niagara River 225 feet above the water between the Canadian and U.S. border. As one official noted, "The plan was to take out a train with passengers on board and the crossing trestle…it was meant to be spectacular and there would have been a lot of carnage."[v]

Origins

The suspects were identified as Chiheb Esseghaier, 35, a Tunisian-born Ph.D. student at a Université du Québec nanotechnology lab, who has been living in Montreal and had studied at the University of Sherbrooke since 2008, and Raed Jaser, 30, of Toronto, who has been living in Canada for twenty years with his family, which was Palestinian by heritage. Though neither man had Canadian citizenship, all of the members of the Jaser family had received Canadian citizenship, other than Raed, whose record of fraud related convictions in Canada prevented him from getting Canadian citizenship.[vi]

Radicalization

In 2004, Canada's Citizenship and Immigration considered deporting Raed, however, instead his family paid a fine and he remained in Canada. However, in the next few years, Raed began to adopt an extremist version of Islam and his father began to worry about the radicalization of his son.[vii]

"He came to me about his son saying how concerned he was getting about the rigidness of his son and his interpretation of Islam. He was becoming self-righteous, becoming pushy, pushing his views on how much they [his family] should be practicing as a Muslim," said Robert Heft.[viii]

Al Qaeda link

Although very little information has been revealed about the travel overseas by Jaser and Esseghaier, Canadian authorities have claimed that the two men received "direction and guidance" from "al Qaeda elements living in Iran," but clarified that there was no evidence that the effort had been sponsored by the government of Iran. Canadian authorities declined to explain how the link to Al Qaeda had been made. One news outlet in Canada, the Canadian Broadcast Network, has claimed that a member of Al-Qaeda living in Iran, on the border with Afghanistan, was guiding and motivating the alleged suspects.[ix]

Project Samossa

In August 2010, Canadian authorities disrupted one of the most peculiar but serious plots in Canada in recent years—also referred to as the *Canadian Idol plot*, since one of the conspirators auditioned for the Canadian Idol TV competition show.

According to security sources, the three conspirators discussed specific targets in Canada may have received some explosives device training overseas. They were charged in with "possessing plans and materials to create makeshift bombs and of being involved in a conspiracy to commit a violent terrorism attack. Among other things, the men had in their possession when arrested—approximately 50 electronic circuit boards, which can be used as remote-control triggers for bombs.[x]

Origins

The three men, Hiva Mohammad Alizadeh, Khurram Sher, and Misbahuddin Ahmed were from Ottawa, Winnipeg, and Montreal, The men were all Canadian citizens, one born and raised in Montreal and the other two having immigrated to Canada at young ages. All three were educated men, pursuing professional careers—one was a graduate of McGill University and an X-ray technologist, another was a pathologist and a third studied to be an electrical engineer. Police allege they were conspiring with others in Afghanistan, Pakistan, Iran, and Dubai, to facilitate terrorist activity.[xi]

Radicalization

To date, Canadian officials and media outlets have not provided much insight on whether and how the men, who were Canadian citizens, radicalized to violence.

Al Qaeda link

The Royal Canadian Mounted Police arrested the men in 2010 and alleged that the men conspired with three other men—who were named and other unnamed individuals in Canada, Iran, Afghanistan, Pakistan, and Dubai as part of their plot. To date, it has not been revealed as to whether any of these linkages were to existing overseas terrorist groups.[xii]

While one member of the trio is alleged to have travelled to the Afghanistan–Pakistan border region and been trained in bomb-making (unclear by whom or which group), another is accused of gathering funds for foreign terror groups that would have been used to buy arms to target Canadian and allied troops in Afghanistan. Neither the RCMP nor CSIS would discuss what motivated the alleged plot or what its targets were, except to say that the group was a threat to the capital region and Canada's national security. However, it has been suggested that the motivation for the attack was Canada's participation in the war in Afghanistan.[xiii]

Project Severe

On March 29, 2011, the RCMP arrested an individual in the Toronto area for terrorism-related offenses. Mohamed Hassan Hersi was arrested and charged for attempting to participate in terrorist activity and for providing counsel to a person to participate in terrorist activity.

The subject was arrested without incident at Toronto Pearson International Airport and it is alleged that he was about to board a plane bound for Cairo, Egypt transiting through London, England, to then go to Somalia with an aim to joining the Al Qaeda affiliate, al Shabaab and to participate in terrorist activities.[xiv]

Origins

Mohamed Hassan Hersi was 25-year-old, who was born in Somalia but moved to Canada as a child. He graduated from University of Toronto with a science degree but was working a job as a security guard. According to many accounts, Hersi had grown frustrated with his life living in a dilapidated public housing unit and tired of watching his mother, a widow who had raised four children alone, struggling to make ends meet. "He was frustrated with his life," the cousin said. "He started saying, 'I'm going to Egypt to get the morals I've lost.' But he never mentioned any of this terrorist thing."[xv]

Radicalization

According to many who knew him, Hersi was a "regular kid" from the West, who loved movies and liked R&B and hip hop, said his cousin. However, it is possible that his frustrations motivated him to explore his religious heritage. A cousin of Hersi's noted that he had heard from other relatives that Hersi was becoming increasingly religious and frequented the Salaheddin Islamic Centre in Scarborough, a mosque where individuals tied to the 2006 Toronto 18 has radicalized. Nevertheless, the cousin noted, "Hersi wasn't radical".[xvi]

While Canadian authorities have not discussed the radicalization to violence of Hersi in any detail, Canadian police and others have expressed concern about the number of young Somali-Canadians who have been recruited, radicalized, and indoctrinated by al-Shabab, which is dedicated to overthrowing Somalia's transitional government. A recent Canadian Security and Intelligence Service (CSIS) report acknowledged several Canadians left for terrorist training camps in Somalia in 2009 from Canada, demonstrating "the attraction for some of travelling abroad for training and becoming ensconced within groups coordinating and planning violent 'jihad' against the West."[xvii]

Al Qaeda links

Al Shabaab, the group that Hersi was potentially volunteering to join is a group in Somalia that is officially allied with Al-Qaeda and has called for terrorist attacks in Canada and a host of other countries.

United Kingdom

The UK has seen its share of Al Qaeda associated or inspired plots since September 2001. In fact, no Western country has been targeted as frequently as the UK by both Al Qaeda directed and inspired plots as the UK. Some of this may be due to the familial links that many south Asian families still have to Kashmir and other areas of conflict in Pakistan. The deadliest plot was clearly the July 7, 2005, London metro bombings that killed 52, but there were equally if not more lethal plots that were disrupted or failed like the July 21, 2005 metro bombing attempt as well as the 2006 transatlantic airlines plot which was disrupted. Though the tempo of terrorist operations against the UK has slowed since 2006, since 2010, there have been some very serious plots which include:

London Stock Exchange Plot

On December 30, 2010, three groups of arrests occurred in the UK in Cardiff, Stoke-on Trent and London. The nine individuals, ranging in age from 19 to 28 years plotted to launch a Christmas bomb attack on the London Stock Exchange, Big Ben, the American embassy, and the home of London Mayor Boris Johnson. In the fall of 2010, two of the men conducted a surveillance trip around central London and also talked about launching a Mumbai-style attack on Parliament. They were also in the process of building pipe bombs based on instructions from the on-line magazine, *Inspire*.[xviii]

Origins

All nine men, who are of Bangladeshi origin and between the ages of 19 and 28, lived in the UK. Seven out of the nine men were born in the UK and the other arrived at much younger ages. "The plotters met through membership of various extremist Islamist groups and stayed in touch over the internet, through mobile phones and at specially arranged meetings—held in parks in a bid to make surveillance difficult. It is understood that some of the Stoke group had been planning to travel to Pakistan to a training camp with the aim of developing a long-term plot, probably within the UK."[xix]

Radicalization

Since the men plead guilty to the charges, only limited information is available on their processes of radicalization. Law enforcement in the UK has characterized the leaders, Mohammed Chowdhury and Shah Rahman from London and the Cardiff contingent as "more like self-starters who probably held radical views for a long time but had taken the next step after immersing themselves in the philosophy of *Inspire* magazine, which promotes the ideology of Anwar al Awlaki who was an operational leader of Al-Qaeda in the Arabian Peninsula (AQAP). British authorities assert that the men had decided to implement the main idea from recent editions of *Inspire magazine,* which suggested that individuals should "get out there and do it."[xx]

According to one British account, "The nine-strong gang all followed a similar path, from poppy burning and militant preaching to terrorism." Interestingly a number of the men had public profiles as very visible political and religious activists who had had already become known for their violent views and were well known to police.

"The terror cell members started out by distributing extremist leaflets and DVDs outside mosques and regularly set up stalls in Cardiff and Stoke, radicalizing vulnerable members of the community." The men chatted over Paltalk in extremist video chat rooms and were known to be associated with extremist Islamist groups like Al Muhajiroun and its successor organization Islam4UK.[xxi]

Al Qaeda links

It was not believed that the men had any operational connections to any terrorist group overseas. Although the gang in Stoke talked about attacking local pubs and clubs, they had decided to travel abroad to get more training, but were interrupted before they could travel. Al Qaeda's role seems to have only been inspirational in this plot as "al-Qaeda inspired books and leaflets, including instructions on making a pipe bomb, were also uncovered during the counter-terrorism operation".[xxii]

The British Airways Plot

On February 25, 2010, Rajib Karim, an employee of British Airways (BA), was arrested by officers of Scotland Yard's Counter Terrorist Command. Rajib worked in the IT department of BA and although he had a low profile, was in direct contact with Anwar al Awlaki, the operational leader of Al Qaeda in the Arabian Peninsula (AQAP). Together, they contemplated how they could exploit Rajib's position within the airline company to launch a terrorist attack that would involve destroying a flight from the United Kingdom to the United States. He was convicted in February of 2011 on of five counts of engaging in conduct in preparation of acts of terrorism.[xxiii]

Origins

Rajib Karim arrived in the UK from Bangladesh at age 26 in 2006. Unlike many of Al Qaeda's other volunteers from the West, Karim came to the West already radicalized and with the deliberate intention to set out to find a job that would be useful to him to plan terror attacks. From his spot in the IT department of British Airways, he kept a low profile. However, at home, he was busy making violent propagandist videos for proscribed terrorist organization Jamaat -ul Mujahideen Bangladesh (JMB).[xxiv]

Karim also worked with his younger brother Tehzeeb Karim and other associates to raise funds for JMB, Al-Qaeda and other terrorist organizations who were then involved in the insurgent activity in Iraq, in the border areas of Pakistan, Afghanistan, and also in the Yemen.[xxv]

Radicalization

Rajib and Tehzeeb began their turn to violence growing up in Bangladesh as they explored radical Islamist thinking over the internet and in study circles while they were in school. Despite being raised in a wealthy family in Bangladesh they and their friends who were educated at the same private school began to be politically active and supported Jammat-ul Mujahideen Bangladesh (JMB), which fought to establish an Islamic state in the country. The group, banned in both Bangladesh and the UK, launched a violent bombing campaign in 2005—but its leaders were arrested and later executed. Rajib subsequently traveled to the UK in 2006 with his British wife to seek medical attention for their sick young son.[xxvi]

Al Qaeda links

In December 2009, Tehzeeb and two others travelled from Bangladesh to Yemen where they successfully made contact with radical cleric Anwar al Awlaki, and the new division of Al-Qaeda which had established itself there, known as Al-Qaeda in the Arabian Peninsular (AQAP). Tehzeeb put al-Awlaqi in touch with his brother Rajib, prompting an exchange of messages between the radical cleric and the BA worker, as they contemplated how they could exploit Rajib's position within the airline company to launch a terrorist attack.[xxvii]

Rajib volunteered information on how he could cause disruption to BA both operationally and financially, by attacking their computer servers, which he said would ground their entire fleet. He also offered to begin recruiting other people. Karim also attempted to train to join a cabin crew; however, he did not have enough time in service. When that failed, AQAP's operational leader, Al-Awlaqi urged Karim to be patient, to stay in the UK while applying for his UK passport, and not to engage in any activity that would expose him to scrutiny as there was a longer-term goal. He wrote: "Our highest priority is the US. Anything there even on a smaller scale compared to what we may do in the UK, would be our choice. So the question is, with the people you have, is it possible to get a package, or a person with a package on board a flight to the [US]...". So, clearly, Rajib Karim, who volunteered his services to AQAP, was working directly on the group's behalf.[xxviii]

The Birmingham Plot

In September of 2011, 12 men were arrested by British authorities in and around the Birmingham area for conspiring to carry out the most devastating attacks in the UK since the July 7, 2005, bombings. The goal was to explode up to eight homemade bombs in rucksacks in crowded places, essentially emulating the July 7, 2005 attacks. The three leaders of the plot were all British citizens. "The men were still discussing potential targets and weapons when they were arrested in September 2011 as they drove across Birmingham, prosecutors said. From bugged conversations and police questioning, the court heard, the men were known to have discussed using rucksack bombs, rifle attacks on crowded streets and targeted strikes against British soldiers." Three of the men were convicted on terrorism-based offenses and eight other men plead guilty to lesser related charges.[xxix]

Origins

The plotters came from areas in Birmingham that are known for being a stronghold of the hard-line Islamic sect, Deobanism, which began as a fundamentalist revivalist movement against British imperialism in India as well of Kashmiri political and military activism, given that Birmingham is where many people from Kashmir settled. Both movements have in the past been an onramp for individuals who later turned to violence on behalf of Al Qaeda.[xxx]

One of the plot leaders had a religious revival while in university and subsequently gravitated to more extremist clerics. Though he earned a pharmacy degree, he dropped out of pharmacy work to teach at an Islamic high school and college in Birmingham. Another was a university student in information technology who dropped out and came from a family with strong links back to disputed area of Kashmir. A third worked as a receptionist in a gym. The group's chief financier, a law graduate, exploited his position as a volunteer area coordinator for Muslim Aid to steal money from the charity by organizing bogus street bucket collections.[xxxi]

Radicalization

Although not much is known about the path the men took to become aspiring terrorists, the court heard that the leader of the group and his fellow plotters were heavily influenced by the propaganda of Anwar al Awlaki. The Queens Counsel prosecutor, Brian Altman described all the men as having a "shared, identical jihadist mindset" influenced by the Yemen-based hate extremist preached Anwar al Awlaki

Al-Qaeda links

Two of the men, Mr. Naseer and Mr. Khalid, were tracked by the security services leaving Britain and entering terrorist training camps linked to Al Qaeda on the Pakistan–Afghanistan border. The men travelled twice to this region, once in 2009 and once in 2010. During both trips, the men received some type of paramilitary training. While the 2009 trip did not reveal details of the nature of the training and who provided the training, Naseer and Khalid admitted that on the second trip, they received training from the Kashmiri militant Islamic group, Harakat ul Mujahedeen (HuM), which has allied itself with Al-Qaeda. It is unclear how the men linked up with Al-Qaeda, but according to Judge Richard Henriques they did. He noted, "Your plot had the blessing of Al-Qaeda and you intended to further the aims of Al Qaeda," he told him. "Clearly nothing was going to stop you short of intervention of the authorities.[xxxii]

France

France, with its aggressive counterterrorism strategy, has often made terrorism related arrests since 2001 at an early phase when plots were still inchoate. As a result, France has been fortunately spared significant linked or associated plots Al Qaeda plots on its territory beyond micro-conspiracies that were disrupted before targets were chosen. The most significant plot in France, related to Al Qaeda type terrorism, occurred in 2011.

Mohammed Merah Attacks

The deadliest terrorist attacks in France since 1995 occurred in March 2011. On March 11, 2012, in Toulouse and then again on March 15 in Montauban, a total of three French soldiers were shot dead by a man wearing a helmet who arrived and left on a motorized scooter. The first attack was on an off-duty French paratrooper of North African descent on the street, outside of the gym. The second attack, on three off duty soldiers, also of North African descent, happened at an ATM machine. Then, on March 19, four people, including two children, were shot dead at the Ozar Hatorah Jewish day school in Toulouse. The perpetrator was identified as Mohammed Merah, a 23-year-old Frenchman of Algerian extraction. His motives included opposition to French participation in the war in Afghanistan, anti-Semitism, and acting to avenge the deaths of Palestinian children killed in Gaza. Mr. Merah was killed after a 30-hour standoff when security officers raided his apartment in Toulouse.

Origins

Mohammed Merah was born in France to French parents of Algerian descent, as one of five children. When his parents divorced, he was five and subsequently, he was raised by his mother in a tough part of Toulouse. During his youth he was arrested many times for petty crime such as purse snatching and ultimately served two prison terms, first for robbery and second for thefts and driving offenses. As a youth he was described as violent and someone with behavioral problems who the police were constantly in contact with.[xxxiii]

Merah also had a history of psychiatric problems and attempted to commit suicide by hanging in 2008 before he attempted to join the French Army twice but was rejected. After a failed attempt to join the French Foreign Legion, and by 2010, Merah began to investigate religion and traveled to Egypt to learn Arabic and then subsequently also went to Pakistan in 2010 and 2011.[xxxiv]

Merah had reportedly split from his wife days before the shootings. He was unemployed at the time of the shootings after having worked as a mechanic.[xxxv]

Radicalization

During the siege of Merah's apartment he told French authorities that it was during one of his stints in prison in 2009 that he became more religious and politicized. After his release, Merah dabbled with relationships with Islamists. Court documents which have redacted information from the French intelligence services note that over time he became involved in the *"Salafist movement Toulouse"*. However, in other French accounts Merah was more difficult to classify in terms of his level of religiosity, as, "sometimes Merah wore a beard, and sometimes shaved it off. Sometimes he seemed devout to friends; at other times he'd go clubbing, staying out to listen to *raï*, popular Arab music." Subsequently, he traveled to Afghanistan and Pakistan on his own where he claimed he received paramilitary training in Waziristan from Al Qaeda.[xxxvi]

Al Qaeda links

Mohamed Merah was in many ways the ultimate Al Qaeda volunteer—born in the West, radicalized in the West, but then traveled to Afghanistan and Pakistan as a volunteer for the cause and to get training and then acted in the name of Al Qaeda. Thus, it is not surprising that Interior Minister Claude Guéant said that Mr. Merah told the police that he called himself one of the "mujahedeen" and claimed to be a member of Al Qaeda. However, there was no Al Qaeda recruiter to catalyze this process but rather as Jean-Louis Bruguière, a former French counterterrorism judge and expert on European terrorism noted, "He appears to be part of the new generation of Islamic terrorists who act alone, abetted by jihadi Web sites and their own anger."[xxxvii]

United States

Although the United States had seen few if any homegrown, Al Qaeda inspired plots in the immediate years after September 2001, the plot against Fort Dix, which was thwarted in April of 2007, heralded a wave of plots, arrests, and even some successful attacks among wannabe Al Qaeda volunteers in the United States. Although this wave crested by the end of 2010, since then there have been some consequential plots and arrests which were punctuated by the deadly Marathon Bombing in Boston on April 15, 2013, which killed four and wounded more than 250.

Some of the American Al Qaeda volunteers who either planned to act at home or abroad between 2007 and 2010 without direct links to overseas terrorist organizations included, the "Fort Dix Six" conspirators' attempt to attack that base in New Jersey, Carlos Bledsoe's June 2009 shooting of Little Rock, AK military recruiting station, which killed one, Major Nidal Hasan's attack on soliders in Fort Hood, which killed 13 and injured 29, and the case of Sharif Mobley, an American man formerly employed at nuclear power plants in New Jersey, who was arrested in 2010 in Yemen on suspicion of being associated with an unnamed terrorist group within the Arabian Peninsula (possibly Al Qaeda of the Arabian Peninsula).

Other cases involved Americans who either attempted to or were successful in linking up with Al Qaeda affiliated groups overseas and either decided to fight abroad or return to the United States to conduct a plot against America. Some of the more prominent of these cases include Omar Hammami, who traveled abroad and joined Al Shabab in Somalia, the five U.S. citizens from the Washington DC area who traveled to Pakistan with the intention of joining a jihadist group, but were instead arrested in Pakistan, Najibullah Zazi, and his two associates, who traveled to Pakistan, linked up with Al Qaeda Core and were involved with an attempt to detonate bombs within the New York City subway system in September 2009 and Faisal Shehzad, who had only recently received U.S. citizenship before he traveled to Pakistan to volunteer to join Tekerek-e-Taliban, the Pakistani Taliban, and then subsequently returned to New York City in May 2010 and attempted to explode a vehicle in Times Square in May 2010.

Three examples of American volunteers to "Al Qaeda" since 2010 worth discussing in further detail include: the case of the Boston Marathon bombers, Jose Pimintel and Samir Khan and Anwar al Awlaki—Americans who joined AQAP.

Americans in Al Qaeda of the Arabian Peninsula

On September 30, 2011, both Samir Khan and Anwar al Awlaki were killed in a drone strike in the Al Jawf governorate of Yemen. While the strike targeted Awalaki, who had become Al Qaeda in the Arabian Peninsula's (AQAP) head of External Operations, Khan was killed by accident. These two men with American citizenship, volunteers to al Qaeda, had arrived in Yemen from the United States, joined the group and were at war with the country in which they both had citizenship—Awlaki had been played a critical role in the attempted Christmas Day Underwear Bombing attack in December of 2009.

Origins

Samir Khan was born in Riyadh, Saudi Arabia, to parents of Pakistani descent and grew up in Queens, New York. He also spent some of his teenage years living in Westbury, New York. He wrote for the high school newspaper, participated in cheerleading, and was an active member of the glee club.[xxxviii]

Anwar al Awlaki Al-Awlaki was born in New Mexico in the United States in 1971 to parents from Yemen, while his father was doing graduate work at U.S. universities. His father, Nasser al-Awlaki, was a Fulbright Scholar. In 1978, when al-Awlaki was seven years old, he returned with his family to Yemen. He lived in Yemen for 11 years, and then returned to the U.S. state of Colorado to attend college. He earned a B.S. in Civil Engineering from Colorado State University (1994), where he was president of the Muslim Student Association.[xxxix]

Radicalization

However, after high school, Khan began to adopt a more fundamentalist version of Islam and created a blog called "InshallahShaheed" or "A martyr, God willing" from his parents' basement in North Carolina. He subsequently started an online magazine which would presage his involvement with *Inspire* magazine. This was called *Jihadi Recollections* and also endorsed violent jihad against the West. After moving to Yemen in 2009 he became the editor of *Inspire*. In an article written by Khan and published in *Inspire* titled "I am proud be a traitor to America", Khan outlined his grievances against the United States.[xl]

Meanwhile, Awlaki worked as an imam in Denver and then San Diego during the 1990s. While his worldview during this period was Islamist in nature, he did not openly espouse violence against the United States. That said, he was interviewed at least four times by the FBI in relation to his links to some of the 9/11 hijackers who lived in San Diego. Subsequently, he moved to the Washington DC area and served as an imam in the Dar al Hijra mosque in Virginia between 2001 and 2002 before leaving the United States for the United Kingdom. As part of his lectures in in December 2002 and January 2003 at the London Masjid al-Tawhid mosque, Awlaki began describing the rewards martyrs receive in paradise, and developing a following among ultraconservative young Muslims, suggesting a turn towards endorsing violence.[xli]

Al Qaeda links

In 2004, Awlaki returned to Yemen and was arrested in 2006 for supposedly participating in an Al Qaeda plot to kidnap a U.S. military official. After his release in late 2007, he went into hiding and likely linked up with AQAP at that point. In January of 2009 he released his essay, *44 Ways to Support Jihad* and by December 2009, Awlaki was on the Yemeni government's most-wanted list and most importantly, involved operationally with the launch of the AQAP Christmas Day Underwear Bomber Plot against Northwest flight 253 to Detroit as a full fledged member of the Yemeni Al Qaeda affiliate.

Meanwhile, after attending Central Piedmont Community College in North Carolina, Samir Khan left the country for Yemen in 2009. His parents, who had not agreed with Khan's views, had attempted an intervention with local religious authorities, but that did not work. After arriving in Yemen, Khan had become an important information arm and a member of Yemen's branch of Al Qaeda—AQAP. Khan began to publish the influential online magazine, *Inspire Magazine*. He proclaimed, in an early edition of the Qaeda magazine, "I am proud to be a traitor,"[xlii]

Returning Servicemen Plot

Jose Pimentel, a native of the Dominican Republic and convert to Islam, was arrested and charged with plotting to detonate bombs in and around New York City in November 2011. He used instructions on how to build a bomb published by A-Qaeda's *Inspire* magazine." After a two and half year investigation, Pimentel was caught while assembling three bombs. In fact, holes had been drilled into pipes, sulfur had been scraped off matches, nails were ready to be used as shrapnel, and wires were used to fashion an ignition device. His targets included members of the Armed Forces who were returning from service in Iraq and Afghanistan.[xliii]

Origins

Pimentel was born in the Dominican Republic and came to the United States at age eight and subsequently became an American citizen. After moving to Schenectady in 2004, New York, he converted to Islam and subsequently went by the name Muhammed Yusef. In December 2005, he was arrested for buying a computer with stolen credit card information he got while working at a Circuit City in Albany, New York.[xliv]

Radicalization

Pimentel seems to have self-radicalized via the Internet. He spent much of his time on the Internet and maintained a radical website on Youtube called TrueIslam1. The website contains a link to the bomb-making article in *Inspire* magazine. Pimentel was also a follower of the Islamist group, Revolution Muslim, which maintained an extremist website. Pimentel corresponded with Jesse Morton, the founder of the website, who was sentenced in June 2012 to 11.5 years in prison for using the internet to solicit violence against individuals to include the writers of the popular TV-satire South Park. One year before he embarked on his plot, during an interview with police, Pimentel defended Osama bin Laden and Anwar al Awlaki as great lecturers and said the Times Square bomber and Major Nidal Hasan who shot dozens of people at Fort Hood in Texas were fighting for a cause, and should not be considered terrorists.[xlv]

Al Qaeda links

Pimentel considered traveling to Yemen to participate in terrorist training and claimed to have emailed radical Yemeni-American cleric Anwar al Awlaki but received no response. As a result, his decision to construct explosive devices and begin a bombing campaign against returning U.S. soldiers happened in the context of Pimentel's desire to act on behalf of Al Qaeda, a volunteer for the cause.[xlvi]

The Boston Marathon Attack

On April 15, 2013, two improvised explosive devices detonated at the Boston Massacre, killing three spectators and injuring more than 250 people. The marathon bombs were constructed largely according to instructions in *Inspire* magazine. In a subsequent event, later that week, an off duty MIT police officer was killed by the two men responsible for the terrorist attack—Tamerlan and Dzhohkar Tsarnaev.

Origins

Born seven years apart in different republics of the former Soviet Union, the Tsarnaev brothers were of Chechen and Dagestani descent. They immigrated to the United States as refugees in 2002. Tamerlan was an aspiring boxer, while Dzhokhar was a student at University of Massachusetts Dartmouth who became a naturalized U.S. citizen on September 11, 2012, seven months before the bombings. "In 2009, Tamerlan won the New England Golden Gloves championship in the 201-pound division, which qualified him for the national tournament in Salt Lake City in May."[xlvii]

Radicalization

After 2010, Tamerlan's religious identification grew stronger, he dropped out of community college, lost interest in boxing and also in music -- "he used to play piano and violin, classical music and rap." Dzhokhar reportedly also admitted to authorities that he and his brother were radicalized, at least in part, by watching Anwar al Awlaki lectures. The Russian investigative newspaper *Novaya Gazeta* reported that during a six-month trip that Tamerlan took to Russia, Tamerlan had sought to join the Muslim insurgency in

Dagestan and had been "in contact with several rebels who were killed by Russian authorities in late spring of 2012 while he was staying in Makhachkala, the regional capital." If this account is accurate, Tamerlan arrived in Russia already radicalized to violence. While his activities in Russia are still being investigated, it appears that he did not join any fighting group and subsequently returned back to Boston. What is unknown is whether he received any paramilitary or bomb making training or not.[xlviii]

Al Qaeda links

Though it is still unclear if Tamerlan linked up with any overseas groups associated with Al Qaeda in Russia, no group has taken responsibility for the attack in Boston. The likelihood is that Tamerlan and Dzhokhar were acting alone, inspired by Al Qaeda's ideology and literally *Inspire* magazine. In fact, as Dzhokhar was hiding in a boat in Watertown, he scribbled notes that suggested that the attack in Boston was "retribution U.S. military action in Afghanistan and Iraq, and called the Boston victims collateral damage in the way Muslims have been in the American-led wars." These grievances, if they were the motivating factors—a more linked to Al Qaeda's worldview than any particular Chechen or Dagestani local grievance.[xlix]

Conclusions

In a sampling of Western countries, Canada, the UK, France and the United States, Al Qaeda type terrorism has not disappeared since 2010. In general, it has become more disconnected from Al Qaeda Core in Afghanistan/Pakistan and when a foreign group has been involved, it is more likely to be with an Al Qaeda affiliate or ally in North Africa, Yemen, or Somalia.

Since 2010, most of the cases involving Western countries, have involved citizens of those very countries who either have radicalized and then mobilized to violence in the West or individuals who traveled or attempted to travel abroad to a zone of conflict to fight there and may or may not have returned to the West to carry out their attack.

Either way, most of the men who have made up Al Qaeda's Volunteer Corps since 2010, have spent time in the West and both have Western origins and in some way have targeted Western targets.

This phenomenon continues to surprise media and Western audiences—many are still shocked when two Canadians turn up in Algeria leading an attack against an energy facility, working with Al Qaeda in the Islamic Maghreb or when two men who were generally raised in Boston, attack their neighbors at the Boston Marathon. However, for counterterrorism practitioners, this threat is not new and remains one of the most difficult to detect. Unfortunately, it does not seem like it will abate any time soon, regardless of the death of Osama bin Laden, leaving challenges from a security, law enforcement, intelligence, and civil liberties perspective that the radicalization to violence and threat that these Western volunteers present, balanced against the need to maintain civil liberties.

Notes

[i] http://www.cbc.ca/news/canada/story/2013/04/04/algeria-canadians-al-qaeda-rcmp.html

[ii] http://www.nytimes.com/2012/07/28/world/middleeast/jeroen-oerlemans-john-cantile-two-journalists-freed-by-islamic-fighters-in-syria-after-weeklong-ordeal.html
http://www.guardian.co.uk/uk/2012/oct/16/charged-kidnap-british-journalist-syria

[iii] http://www.eitb.com/fr/infos/societe/detail/854031/fusillades-operation-policiere-toulouse/

[iv] Almost 12 years after the attacks of September 11, 2001, the very definition of what Al Qaeda as an organization is and what type of threat it represents have evolved to a point where clarification and definition are required before even beginning the discussion. For the benefit of this article, a broad definition of "Al Qaeda", referring to a loose global alliance of like-minded Sunni jihadist terrorist organizations that may share affinity, an alliance, operational coordination, and/or personnel/weapons and are intent on attacking Western interests both locally and abroad under the banner "Al Qaeda", will serve as the definition of the group, rather than the more narrowly defined "Al Qaeda Core, whose presence was generally limited to Afghanistan, Pakistan, and Yemen.

[v] http://www.dailymail.co.uk/news/article-2313517/Canada-terror-plot-First-picture-Chiheb-Esseghaier-revealed-Toronto-Muslim-leader-tipped-authorities.html

[vi] http://news.nationalpost.com/2013/04/24/na0425-sb-terror-2/
http://news.nationalpost.com/2013/04/22/canadian-terrorist-plot-was-planned-by-chiheb-esseghaier-raed-jaser/

[vii] http://globalnews.ca/news/511849/prior-fraud-conviction-almost-led-to-deportation-of-one-via-rail-terror-suspect/

[viii] http://www.cleveland.com/world/index.ssf/2013/04/canadian_terror_suspect_had_ra.html

[ix] http://www.cbc.ca/news/canada/story/2013/04/23/via-terror-plot-suspects-broader-network.html

[x] http://www.cbc.ca/news/canada/story/2010/08/27/f-terrorism-charges-august-2010.html

[xi] http://www.csmonitor.com/World/Americas/2010/0827/Canada-arrests-of-citizens-raise-concerns-of-homegrown-terrorism

[xii] http://www.cbc.ca/news/canada/story/2010/08/27/f-terrorism-charges-august-2010.html
http://www.actforcanada.ca/rcmp-say-homegrown-terror-suspects-preparing-to-build-ieds/

[xiii] http://m.theglobeandmail.com/news/national/terror-plot-would-have-brought-afghan-war-home-to-canada/article1378378/?service=mobile

[xiv] http://www.rcmp-grc.gc.ca/on/news-nouvelles/2011/11-03-30-gta-rgt-inset-eisn-eng.htm

[xv] http://www.thestar.com/news/crime/2011/03/31/u_of_t_graduates_arrest_on_terror_charges_alarms_toronto_somalis.html

[xvi] http://www.thestar.com/news/crime/2011/03/31/u_of_t_graduates_arrest_on_terror_charges_alarms_toronto_somalis.html

[xvii] http://www.theglobeandmail.com/news/national/terror-suspect-nabbed-at-toronto-airport-going-directly-to-trial/article1357707/

[xviii] http://www.telegraph.co.uk/news/uknews/terrorism-in-the-uk/9053681/Terrorists-admit-plot-to-bomb-London-Stock-Exchange-and-US-Embassy.html

xix http://www.guardian.co.uk/uk/2012/feb/01/terror-plotters-mumbai-attacks-london

xx http://www.dailymail.co.uk/news/article-2094799/London-Stock-Exchange-bomb-plot-4-radical-Muslims-planned-target-Boris-Johnson.html#ixzz2S4Gzte8Q

xxi Ibid.

xxii http://www.guardian.co.uk/uk/2012/feb/01/terror-plotters-mumbai-attacks-london and http://www.telegraph.co.uk/news/uknews/terrorism-in-the-uk/9053681/Terrorists-admit-plot-to-bomb-London-Stock-Exchange-and-US-Embassy.html

xxiii http://content.met.police.uk/News/Man-jailed-for-30-years-for-terrorism-offences/1260268719101/1257246745756

xxiv http://content.met.police.uk/News/Man-jailed-for-30-years-for-terrorism-offences/1260268719101/1257246745756

xxv Ibid.

xxvi http://www.bbc.co.uk/news/uk-12573824

xxvii http://content.met.police.uk/News/Man-jailed-for-30-years-for-terrorism-offences/1260268719101/1257246745756

xxviii http://content.met.police.uk/News/Man-jailed-for-30-years-for-terrorism-offences/1260268719101/1257246745756

xxix http://www.nytimes.com/2013/02/22/world/europe/3-convicted-in-britain-over-terrorist-plot.html

xxx http://raffaellopantucci.com/

xxxi Ibid.

xxxii http://www.latimes.com/news/world/worldnow/la-fg-wn-britain-terrorist-plot-20130426,0,1479785.story
http://raffaellopantucci.com/
http://www.nytimes.com/2013/02/22/world/europe/3-convicted-in-britain-over-terrorist-plot.html

xxxiii "Toulouse Shootings: Merah's Path to Murder", BBC, March 22, 2012

xxxiv Richard Galpin, "French Police Swoop Nets Islamist Militant Suspects," *Sydney Morning Herald*, March 31, 2012 and Oliver Moore, "Mohammed Merah: Petty Criminal, Part-time Jihadist, Polite but a Loner", *Globe and Mail,* March 21, 2012.

xxxv Dan Bilefsky and Maia de la Baume, "French Gunman Seen as Homegrown Militant," The New York Times, March 21, 2012.

xxxvi "Mohamed Merah était "en phase de radicalisation" dès janvier 2011," Le Monde, August 9, 2012 and Oliver Moore, "Mohammed Merah: Petty Criminal, Part-time Jihadist, Polite but a Loner", *Globe and Mail*, March 21, 2012.

xxxvii Dan Bilefsky and Maia de la Baume, "French Gunman Seen as Homegrown Militant," The New York Times, March 21, 2012.

xxxviii Timothy Bolger, "Slain al Qaeda Mouthpiece Samir Khan's Westbury Roots," Long Island Press, October 6, 2011.

xxxix Scott Shane, Mekhennet Souad, "Anwar al-Awlaki—From Condeming Terror to Preaching Jihad," *The New York Times*, May 1, 2010.

xl http://www.cnn.com/2010/US/07/18/al.qaeda.magazine/index.html

xli Susan Schmidt, "Imam From Va. Mosque Now Thought to Have Aided Al-Qaeda," *The Washington Post,* November 20, 2009 and Scott Shane, Mekhennet Souad, "Anwar al-Awlaki – From Condeming Terror to Preaching Jihad," *The New York Times*, May 1, 2010.

xlii Suzanne Kelly, "Proud to be an American Traitor," CNN, October 1, 2011

xliii http://www.nyc.gov/html/nypd/html/pr/plots_targeting_nyc.shtml

[xliv] http://www.nydailynews.com/news/crime/terror-suspect-jose-pimentel-mom-city-police-article-1.980715

[xlv] Joseph Goldstein, "Documents Show Extent of F.B.I.'s Role in Terror Case," *The New York Times*, November 13, 2012 and Ibid.

[xlvi] http://www.nyc.gov/html/nypd/html/pr/plots_targeting_nyc.shtml

[xlvii] Deborah Sontag, David M. Herszenhorn and Serge F. Kovaleski, "A Battered Dream and then a Violent Path," *The New York Times*, April 27, 2013.

[xlviii] Scott Shane and David M. Herszenhorn, "Agents Pore Over Suspect's Trip to Russia," *The New York Times*, April 27, 2013

[xlix] "Boston Bombings Suspect Dzhokhar Tsarnaev Left Note in Boat He Hid In," *CBS News.com*, May 17, 2013

About the Author

Mitchell D. Silber serves as Executive Managing Director of K2 Intelligence, and was the Director of Intelligence Analysis for the NYPD from 2007 to 2012.

International Journal on Criminology—Volume 1—Number 1—Fall 2013

Criminal State and Illicit Economy: A Game Changer for the XXIst Century - Crime, illegal trades, economy and state

Mickaël R. Roudaut

Taking advantage of globalization, crime and criminal markets grew to become, beyond *public security*[1], a question of *global and national security*[2] influencing international relations, economy and society as a whole. Moreover, the classic divide between state and organised crime, the former fighting the latter, is now longer the single rule of the game.

Nowadays, in many countries and areas within them, organised crime and state interests, closely intertwined, cannot be distinguished. To the point that the state no longer seeks to eradicate or reduce the organized crime pressure but aims to control trafficking rings for its economic, personal and partners benefits.

Furthermore, the millions of employees of the illicit economy producing counterfeits, smuggling hundreds of thousands of migrants, harvesting coca leaves or scratching poppy fields, poaching elephant or tiger carcasses and pursuing the laundering of the proceeds in the licit economy on one side and the millions more buying contraband cigarettes, smoking cannabis, paying for sex from coerced women or employing irregular migrants on the other, create a vast global market. Given its scale and profitability, this illicit economy became an alternative and suppletive model of development closely intertwined with the legal sphere.

Yet, such awareness tends to remain confined to some academic spheres instead of being fully acknowledged within international relations, political economy and geopolitics so as to be translated at policy making level.

That is why the traditional notions of organized crime, corruption and penetration of public bodies no longer suffice to fully embrace and understand the modern relations between crime, illegal trades, economy and state. Geocriminology[3], the geopolitics of illicit, aims to expose this reality and impacts.

---

[1] To public, property and business.

[2] To sovereignty, government and economic and global stability.

[3] Geocriminology (neologism from the author) studies the rivalries of power within a given territory in its political, social, economic, geographic and perceived dimensions (i.e. the emotional and spiritual dimension of a territory forging the Nation and by extension what is rightfully 'mine' e.g. Los Angeles gang outbursts, Mexican cartels confrontation…) through interactions between illicit flows, their actors and the legal sphere. It also covers the use of illicit means by legal actors. These actions, inherently illegal but considered legitimate, are covered by the reason of state. Mickaël R. Roudaut, *Marchés criminels – un acteur global*, PUF, coll. Questions judiciaires, May 2010, 304 p, 'Géopolitique de l'illicite', *Diplomatie* n° 50 May-Jun. 2011, 'Géopolitique de la crise, des monnaies et de la fraude', *Diplomatie* n° 55, Mar-Apr. 2012, 'Géopolitique de l'illicite : une nouvelle grammaire' in *Géographie des conflits* (Dir. Béatrice Giblin), La Documentation française, May 2012, p. 40-1, '*In Narco Veritas*? Géocriminologie du Mexique et de sa région. Marchés criminels, économie et État', *Sécurité Globale* n° 21, automn 2012, 'Sécurité intérieure et crime organisé au XXIe siècle : un essai de typologie' in *Regard croisés sur la sécurité intérieure*, to be published and *Géopolitique des marchés criminels*, to be published.

Crime is shaping the world

Since the end of the Cold War, an unprecedented openness in trade, travel, communication and finance has created an equally unprecedented era of economic growth and technological innovation, for the benefit of both citizens and consumers. Yet, as global governance struggles to keep pace with this destruction of barriers, massive criminal opportunities have emerged that exploit the open market economy.

Indeed, transnational organized crime changed in five defining ways. First, from mono-activity centered on drug trafficking, it expanded its reach to illicit entrepreneurship investing in various criminal trades (counterfeiting, cigarettes or migrants) and smuggling of all kinds once the routes and logistics in place.

Second, from a centralized and vertical model, criminal groups evolved in amorphous, loose, adaptable and flat transnational networks. Should a cell or some members be identified and arrested, the overall network would reconfigure itself almost naturally.

Third, criminal groups, following on the logic of illicit entrepreneurship, refined their *modi operandi* from expertise in passing borders to penetration of the licit economy through gained stakes and influence over strategic markets[4] (natural resources, energy, waste, financial sector) while taking advantage of new technologies to access information, conceal their identity and reduce detection risk.

Fourth, the long-time barrier between organized crime and terrorism fell. Nowadays, a blend of insurgency, crime and terrorism is at play whether in Sahel, Af-Pak border or in the more classical example of the Andean forests (FARC[5], ELN[6], *Sendero luminoso*[7]). Many terrorist groups, no longer or less state sponsored while in need of sustainable and discreet source of income, turned to criminal markets (notably counterfeiting, cigarette and drugs). Hezbollah[8], Abu Sayyaf Group, Al Qaeda's Affiliates such as Al-Qaeda in Islamic Maghreb or Haqqani Network, PKK[9], Hamas, Islamic Jihad, terrorist movements in Northern Ireland, Kosovo or Chechen separatists to name a few, have been or are considered engaged in organized crime-type activities[10]. This crime-terror nexus does not limit itself to terrorism turning to organized crime but concerns the adoption of terror tactics by criminals as well. The filming of executions, amputations, decapitations and hangings by Mexican criminal groups corresponds to the classic strategy of tension aiming to attract Mexico in the cycle of repression-vengeance, with the prospects of police blunders (extra-judicial killings), that would undermine the legitimacy of the

---

[4] See *infra*.

[5] *Fuerzas Armadas Revolucionarias de Colombia*/ Revolutionary Armed Forces of Colombia.

[6] *Ejército de Liberación Nacional*/National Liberation Army.

[7] Shining Path.

[8] In March 2006, the U.S. Federal Bureau of Investigation (FBI) busted a global network of counterfeit medicine fuelling Hezbollah with branches stretching from Brazil to China through Canada and Lebanon. More recently, for the U.S. Treasury Department, the "*Lebanese Canadian Bank – through management complicity, failure of internal controls, and lack of application of prudent banking standards – has been used extensively by persons associated with an international drug trafficking and money laundering network to move hundreds of millions of dollars monthly in cash proceeds... - as much as $200 million per month - ... from illicit drug sales into the formal financial system*". Hezbollah benefited from these funds.

[9] *Partiya Karkerên Kurdistan*/ Kurdistan Workers' Party.

[10] European Parliament, *Europe's crime-terror nexus: Links between terrorist and organised crime groups in the European Union*, 2012, 65 p., and CRS, *Terrorism and Transnational Crime: Foreign Policy Issues for Congress*, 19 Oct. 2012, 40 p.

state[11]. Violence is therefore political. The D-Company, a criminal organization first invested in smuggling activities (1970s), evolved in a fully fledged organized crime group also engaged in insurgency-terrorism through "*supporting efforts to smuggle weapons to militant and terrorist groups*". "*By the 1990s, it began to conduct and participate in terrorist attacks, including the March 12, 1993, Bombay bombing*"[12].

Fifth, in many countries and regions within them, crime and state merged to give rise to a new type of organized crime entity, the criminal state.

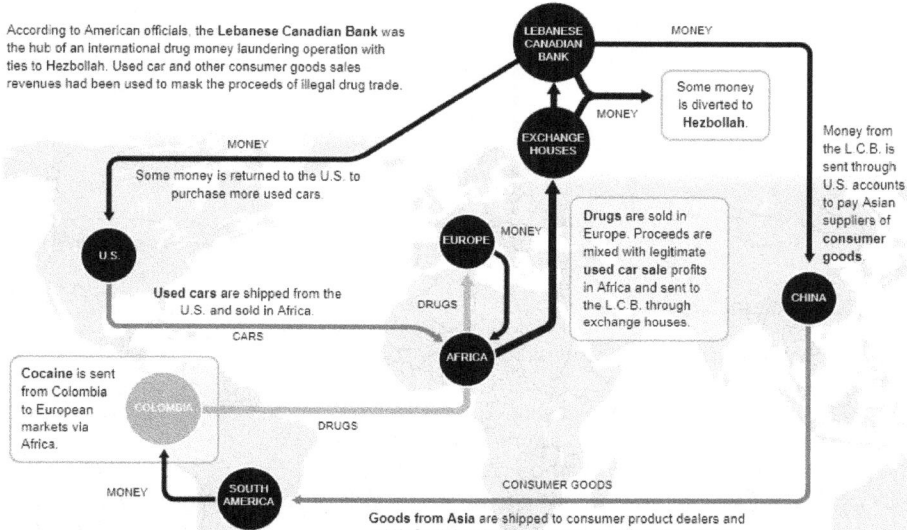

According to American officials, the **Lebanese Canadian Bank** was the hub of an international drug money laundering operation with ties to Hezbollah. Used car and other consumer goods sales revenues had been used to mask the proceeds of illegal drug trade.

Some money is returned to the U.S. to purchase more used cars.

Used cars are shipped from the U.S. and sold in Africa.

Cocaine is sent from Colombia to European markets via Africa.

Some money is diverted to Hezbollah.

Money from the L.C.B. is sent through U.S. accounts to pay Asian suppliers of consumer goods.

Drugs are sold in Europe. Proceeds are mixed with legitimate **used car sale** profits in Africa and sent to the L.C.B. through exchange houses.

Goods from Asia are shipped to consumer product dealers and sold in South America in a scheme to pay off cocaine suppliers.

Hezbollah: a terrorist organization turned criminal group through the Lebanese Canadian Bank case   Source: *New York Times*, 13 December 2011

Every year, hundreds of billions of dollars are produced by the illicit trades and are essentially laundered in the licit economy[13], dozens of conflicts are fuelled by the smuggling of small arms and light weapons, digital piracy, in less than a decade, transformed the movie and music industries and on average, 7 500 illicit drug-induced deaths occur in the EU and Norway. This influence on society, by all account, is found more lasting than any terrorist attacks.

Of course, criminal groups rip the benefits from these illegal trades to finance necessary work force and protection from lawful authorities (corruption), to the point of competing with states in both 'monopol[ies] of the legitimate violence' (Weber)[14] and taxation (through extortion).

This contributes to the burgeoning of so-called 'failed states', or more eloquently said, sovereignty without power, along major illicit flows routes. The global and local impacts of the criminal economy, from the Andean forest to French suburbs and North America through West Africa and Central America, leave no country immune.

---

[11] Mickaël R. Roudaut, *In Narco Veritas?*, op. cit.

[12] CRS, *Terrorism and Transnational Crime*, op. cit.

[13] For the UNODC, criminals, especially drug traffickers, may have laundered around US$ 1.6 trillion, or 2.7 % of global GDP, in 2009. See *infra*.

[14] For a case-study, see Mickaël R. Roudaut, *In Narco Veritas*? op. cit.

Indeed, this pervasiveness concerns developed countries as well. After all among the ten mafia-type organizations, seven find their origins in G8 countries[15].

Nature of Transnational Organized Crime	
1990s and Earlier	**Current Patterns**
Centralized hierarchical structures	Loose, amorphous, highly adaptable networks
Limited use of information technology	Increasing role of cyber capabilities in illicit activities
Illicit activities dominant	Legitimate business mixed with illicit activity
Clear separation of drug trafficking and other organized criminal activities	Non-drug-producing groups now trafficking
Cash-based local enterprises	Global investments and use of financial infrastructures

National Security Implications	
1990s and Earlier	**Current Patterns**
Domestic and regional scope	Transnational and global scope
Influenced some states' behavior	Co-opting, undermining some states or instruments of state power
Isolated links to terrorists	Offering services to foreign terrorist organizations
Targeting and enforcement easier than today	Adaptability outpacing targeting and enforcement

Source: U.S. Office of the Director of National Intelligence, *The threat to US national security posed by transnational organised crime,* 2011

Beyond, the confusion between state and crime concerns not only countries stranded on corruption reefs, hostages of the narco-economy or in the midst of a political turmoil, or all the above united in a perfect storm (Afghanistan).

"It is impossible to understand all the workings that govern prices, intermediaries or the structure of supply networks of Russian gas that arrives in Europe (transiting notably by Ukraine) without taking into account the role of organized crime"[16].

Illustration of this quantum leap from public security to global and national security concerns, an alleged criminal, present on the FBI ten most wanted fugitives list for being suspected of having defrauded investors of more than 150 million dollars from 1993 to 1998 is also and more importantly reputed to be invested in the Eastern European gas market. According to the FBI and the Department of Justice, he *"uses his ill-gotten gains to influence governments and their economies"*[17].

---

[15] Cosa Nostra, Camorra, 'Ndrangheta, Sacra Corona Unita and Stidda in Italy, U.S. Cosa Nostra and Yakusa in Japan. The three remaining being the Triads in China, the Turkish *maffya* and the Albanian-speaking mafia while a scholar debate takes place concerning *vory v zakone* (a part of Russian organized crime) regarding its mafia status. A mafia can be defined as a secret society or an institutionalized association anchored in a territory while having an international and polycriminal activity. Readily compartmentalized and hierarchical even though a looser network of cells can also be used, a genuine mafia is driven by a set of rites (including initiation), rules (omerta ...) and beliefs. Its recruitment is usually based on family and clan. Should all these criteria be met, only the test of time can confer the mafia qualification, hence the debate over *vory v zakone*. For an example of Mafia code of honor see the triads 36 commitments oath, Thierry Cretin, *Mafia (s)*, Chronique editions 2009, p. 124-5.

[16] Moisés Naím, 'La mafia au cœur de l'État', *Slate*, 10 May 2012.

[17] FBI, 'Global Con Artist' Attorney General Michael B. Mukasey, 'Attorney General Michael B. Mukasey Delivers Remarks at the CSIS Forum on Combating International Organized Crime' 23 Apr. 2008, *Political/Congressional Transcript Wire* in CRS, *Organised crime: An evolving challenge for U.S. law enforcement,* 6 Jan. 2012.

In a meeting with the U.S. Ambassador in Kiev, reported in a 2008 diplomatic cable released by WikiLeaks, the nominal owner of the company distributing gas to the EU allegedly "*acknowledged ties to [the] Russian organized crime figure [identified hereabove and present on the FBI ten most wanted list], stating he needed [his] approval to get into business in the first place [...]. He noted that it was impossible to approach a government official for any reason without also meeting with an organized crime member at the same time. [He] acknowledged that he needed, and received, permission from [this Russian organized crime figure] when he established various businesses, but he denied any close relationship to him. If he needed a permit from the government, for example, he would invariably need permission from the appropriate "businessman" who worked with the government official who issued the particular permit. He maintained that the era of the "law of the street" had passed and businesses could now be run legitimately in Ukraine*"[18].

It is thus logically that the 2011 U.S. Strategy to combat transnational organized crime (TOC) considers TOC to be a "*national security threat*" while urging other states to make a similar step[19].

The U.S. President goes on to declare "*Criminal networks are not only expanding their operations, but they are also diversifying their activities, resulting in a convergence of transnational threats that has evolved to become more complex, volatile, and destabilizing. These networks also threaten U.S. interests by forging alliances with corrupt elements of national governments and using the power and influence of those elements to further their criminal activities. In some cases, national governments exploit these relationships to further their interests to the detriment of the United States*"[20].

This last sentence, a rare instance in official publications, underlines the following; governments can, for reason of state or less legitimate motives, protect, take advantage or control and develop criminal activities. This further reveals the geopolitical power of crime and its systemic impact. It notably justifies the shift from public to global and national security concerns.

However, the traditional legal and operational tool box made of treaties, international, regional and bilateral cooperations and organizations appears ill-adapted to this new type of criminal player proven as flexible and agile as organized crime while enjoying the legal privileges and immunities of states.

The inbreeding of organized crime and state: from reason of state to criminal state

Defining trait of the XXIst century, as mentioned in Obama's statement, organized crime can be overtaken by states, not as to be destroyed, but as to be controlled in view to reap the benefit of its illegal deeds.

As any living creature, a state is driven by one paramount instinct; survive and thrive. History shows that no action will be spared to ensure this very survival, including, of course, through actions that would be deemed illegal if not covered by the reason of state. If history has found legitimacy in some of them, nowadays, illegal state actions

---

[18] Cable #002414, 10 Dec. 2008 http://www.guardian.co.uk/world/us-embassy-cables-documents/182121 and cable #002294, 21 Nov. 2008 http://www.guardian.co.uk/world/us-embassy-cables-documents/179510

[19] Following on the 2010 National Intelligence Estimate on international organized crime which first in the U.S.A. made the shift from public security threat to national security threat.

[20] White House, *U.S. Strategy to combat transnational organized crime*, Jun. 2011, p. iii.

involving organized crime no longer seem to be directly led by this survival imperium but rather more economic and prosaic personal financial enrichment. A symbiotic relation between state and crime is thus developed[21].

Bulgaria

Another quantum leap example from public security to global and national security concerns can be found in a now aged 2005 U.S. diplomatic cable released by WikiLeaks. *"TIM [described as the major organized crime group] controls some of the largest quarries of inert materials in Bulgaria, and through its trading company [...] it also has a significant share of the production and trade in fertilizers, petroleum products, and chemicals"*[22].

For the author of the cable *"Organized crime has a corrupting influence on all Bulgarian institutions, including the government, parliament and judiciary. In an attempt to maintain their influence regardless of who is in power, OC [Organized Crime] figures donate to all the major political parties. As these figures have expanded into legitimate businesses, they have attempted -- with some success -- to buy their way into the corridors of power. [...] Below the level of the national government and the leadership of the major political parties, OC "owns" a number of municipalities and individual members of parliament. This direct participation in politics -- as opposed to bribery -- is a relatively new development for Bulgarian OC. At the municipal level, a by-election earlier this year in the town of [...] resulted in the complete takeover of the municipal government by figures who have made little attempt to conceal their links to powerful smuggling interests. Similarly in the regional center of [...], OC figures control the municipal council and the mayor's office. Nearly identical scenarios have played out in half a dozen smaller towns and villages across Bulgaria"*[23].

Italy

Crime and politics in Italy have been extensively reported and studied. The aim is not remind well-known corruption and influence cases but whether *pacta sceleris* reached a level of national security concern.

Key point, notably developed by Umberto Santino, Italian mafias are not always against the state since *"they are 'in' and 'with' the state as well"*[24] through the *'mafia bourgeoisie'*. *"Criminal groups, a few thousand members in total*[25], *interact with a much larger social group within which decision-making power is exercised by illegal actors [...] and by legal actors, professionals, entrepreneurs, public servants, elected politicians and officials in charge of institutions, [forming] a mafia bourgeoisie"*[26].

Criminal powers anchored in a territory (mafias, cartels) possess an electoral power (votes). In 2004, 190 'families' were identified (approximately 5,200 members) in Sicily, among which 89 in the province of Palermo (about 3,200 members)[27]. On average, each

---

[21] Mickaël R. Roudaut, *Sécurité intérieure et crime organisé au XXIe siècle*, op. cit.

[22] Cable #001207, 7 Jul. 2005 http://wikileaks.ch/cable/2005/07/05SOFIA1207.html

[23] *Idem.*

[24] Arles Arloff, 'Italie, un pouvoir corrompu', *Futuribles* #381, Jan. 2012.

[25] Camorra (6,700), 'Ndrangheta (6,000), Cosa Nostra (5,200), Sacra Corona Unita (1,800), Stidda (unknown), represent roughly 'only' 20,000 persons. Their impact cannot be understood without the 'mafia bourgeoisie'. T. Cretin, *Mafia(s)*, op. cit., p. 21, 25, 31, 36, 38-39.

[26] Umberto Santino, *La mafia interpretata Dilemmi, Stereotipi, paradigmi*, Rubbettino editions, 250 p., 1995, p. 145 in Arles Arloff and André-Yves Portnoff, 'La mafia italienne : persistances et résistance' *Futuribles* n° 326, Jan. 2007, p. 32.

[27] T. Cretin, *Mafia(s)*, op. cit., p. 21.

'man of honor' controlling forty to fifty votes, the electoral base of Cosa Nostra in the Palermo province would range from to 128 000 to 160 000 votes[28], enough to mediate the political debate, or even hold its key.

For the anti-mafia deputy prosecutor of Calabria, *"the 'Ndrangheta [...] controls 20% of votes, it is sufficient to switch the majorities in our small towns"*[29]. Criminal powers are thus both fought and courted by law abiding personnel and corruptible individuals.

Unsurprisingly, from July 1991 to February 2008, 172 municipal councils were dissolved for operating under mafia influence[30].

The trial for *'participation in a criminal association'* of a key figure, from the years 1955 to 1992, seven times President of the Council (Prime Minister), Andreotti, leave limited room for speculation on the national security concern reached by organized crime penetration in Italy. The supreme court in its October 2004 ruling declared that *"during the 1970s and through to the spring of 1980, Andreotti enjoyed friendly and direct relations with leading members of Cosa Nostra and had knowingly and deliberately cultivated a stable relationship with Mafiosi.[...] The judgment found that Andreotti had been involved in criminal association until spring of 1980, but the crime was time-barred and insufficient proof brought him acquittal for the time after that"*[31]. In other words, Andreotti was found guilty of criminal association but the expiry of the statute of limitation prevented any sentence. The ruling was translated by the Italian press in a simple acquittal.

Japan

The Japanese situation can be difficult to apprehend for a westerner eye. To the opposite of criminal wisdom, *yakusa* (or *boryokudan*) have offices, give away business cards, may grant interviews and are subject of fan magazines. They can compete with traditional companies in the hiring of graduates straight out of business schools. The relation between state, power and *yakusa* is thus well documented[32].

Comprising roughly 79,000 persons divided among 22 groups (in 2012), they are considered to have played a key role in the decade long recession that hit Japan at the beginning of the 90' to the point that the period is often referred to as the *'Yakusa recession'*[33].

---

[28] According to the *pentito* Antonino Calderone (1987) and Xavier Raufer (http://www.xavier-raufer.com).

[29] *Le Monde,* 7 Nov. 2005.

[30] Italian Parliament, *Relazione annuale della Commissione parlamentare di inchiesta sul fenomeno della criminalità organizzata mafiosa o similare 'ndrangheta',* 2008, p. 116.

[31] David Lane, *Into the heart of the Mafia,* 2010, Profile books LTD, p. 4.

[32] David Kapan and Alec Dubro, *Yakusa,* du Picquier editions, 2002, Thierry Cretin, *Mafia(s),* op. cit., p. 130-141, *Foreign policy,* 'The Yakusa lobby', 13 Dec. 2012.

[33] *Far Eastern Economic Review,* The Yakuza Recession, 17 Jan. 2002: *"Neither Miyawaki nor any other credible commentator suggests that deflation, policy blunders, political inertia and a whole range of other factors haven't contributed to Japan's decade-long stagnation. All the same, Miyawaki, a Tokyo University Law School graduate, former spokesman for Prime Minister Yasuhiro Nakasone and former head of the National Police Agency's organized crime division, estimates that up to 50% of the bad debts held by Japanese banks could be impossible to recover because they involve organized crime and corrupt politicians"*, thus slowing down the decade long recovery process, hence the 'Yakusa recession' moniker.

Illustration of the global and national security concern *yakusa* represent, a 2007 Japan police report warned that "*the yakusa made such incursions into the financial market that they threaten the very basis of the Japanese economy*"[34]. More recently they "*have been tied to a wide range of businesses, including the nuclear industry*[35] *and [...] a Japanese camera manufacturer mired in a major accounting scandal*"[36].

Other illustration of the global reach of *yakusa*, following the Executive Order, issued in 2011 by President Obama to target and disrupt four major transnational criminal organizations (Brother's circle, Eurasian based – Camorra, Italian based – Yakusa and Zetas, Mexican based)[37], the U.S. Treasury announced in February 2012 the freezing of the American-based assets of the *Yamaguchi-gumi*, the larger *yakusa* group, and two of its leaders. It will also bar any transactions between Americans and members of the penalized crime syndicate.

Shaping their image, a classic with mafia-type organizations, *yakusa* "*were some of the first responders after the earthquake [that provoked a tsunami that hit the Fukushima power plant], providing food and supplies to the devastated area and patrolling the streets to make sure no looting occurred*"[38].

			End of 2009	Net change from end of 2008	Share		
Three major groups	The sixth Yamaguchi-gumi	Members	19,000	-1,200	45.0% (members-only share 49.2%)		
		Associates	17,400	-400			
		Total	36,400	-1,600			
	Sumiyoshi-kai	Members	6,100	0	15.8% (members-only share 15.8%)		
		Associates	6,700	+100			
		Total	12,800	+100			
	Inagawa-kai	Members	4,700	-100	11.6% (members-only share 12.2%)		
		Associates	4,700	+200			
		Total	9,400	+100			
Combined total of the three major groups		Members	29,800	-1,300	72.4% (members-only share 77.2%)		
		Associates	28,800	-100			
		Total	58,600	-1,400			
Other		Members	8,800	-500	27.6% (members-only share 22.8 %)		
		Associates	13,500	+200			
		Total	22,300	-300			
All Boryokudan groups combined		Members	38,600	-1,800	100.0%		
		Associates	42,300	+100			
		Total	80,900	-1,700			

Source: Japan National Police Academy, Police Policy Research Center, *Crime in Japan in 2009*

Kosovo

A widely reported Council of Europe report, investigating organ trafficking in Kosovo, adopted by its Parliamentary Assembly in 2011, held the view that "*[...] in confidential reports spanning more than a decade, agencies dedicated to combating drug smuggling in at least five countries have named Hashim Thaqi [Prime Minister of*

---

[34] *Foreign policy,* 'The Yakusa lobby', op. cit.
[35] *The Telegraph,* 'How the Yakuza went nuclear', 21 Feb. 2012.
[36] *New York Times,* 'U.S. Treasury Dept. Penalizes Japan's Largest Organized-Crime Group', 24 Feb. 2012.
[37] Executive order #13581, 24 Jul. 2011.
[38] *The Telegraph,* op. cit.

Kosovo] and other members of his 'Drenica Group' as having exerted violent control over the trade in heroin and other narcotics"[39].

"In the course of the last ten years, intelligence services from several Western European countries, law enforcement agencies, including the Federal Bureau of Investigation (FBI) in the United States, and analysts of several nationalities working within NATO structures have prepared authoritative, well-sourced, corroborated reports on the unlawful activities of this 'Drenica Group'"[40].

"At a minimum, there is solid documentary evidence to demonstrate the involvement of this group, and its financial sponsors, in money laundering, smuggling of drugs and cigarettes, human trafficking, prostitution, and the violent monopolisation of Kosovo's largest economic sectors including vehicle fuel and construction"[41].

Myanmar

Viewed from Bangkok press *"Among the candidates who won in the South-east Asian nation's first election in 20 years on Nov. 7 [2010] are six well-known drug barons. They represented the Union Solidarity and Development Party, the junta's political front, which triumphed comfortably in the poll"*[42].

For the U.S. Department of State *"[Birman] policy of folding ethnic armed groups into quasi [state]-controlled [border guard forces - BGFs] complicates anti-narcotics efforts as BGFs are often complicit, if not active protectors, of illicit drug production and trafficking. [...]. Many inside Burma assume some senior [government] officials benefit financially from narcotics trafficking, but these assumptions have never been confirmed through arrests, convictions, or other public revelations. There were credible reports that mid-level military officers and government officials were engaged in drug-related corruption, however, no military officer above the rank of colonel has ever been charged with drug-related corruption. [...] [Government] officials are likely aware of the cultivation, production, and trafficking of illegal narcotics in areas they control"*[43].

Nicaragua

According to 2006 U.S. diplomatic cables released by WikiLeaks, organized crime and state seemed to have followed a partnership pattern.

"In 1984 Daniel Ortega [at power from 1979 to 1985, Head of state from 1985 to 1990 and since 2007] negotiated a deal with Colombian drug kingpin Pablo Escobar hereby Escobar received refuge for several months in Nicaragua after he had ordered the killing of the Colombian Minister of Justice. At the same time, Escobar's drug trafficking operation received Ortega's approval to land and load airplanes in Nicaragua as they sought to ship cocaine to the United States. In return, Ortega and the FSLN [Sandinista National Liberation Front] received large cash payments from Escobar. Interior Minister [...] and his subordinates went so far as to assist Escobar with the loading and unloading of drugs onto his airplanes in Nicaragua. The Drug Enforcement Agency (DEA)

---

[39] Council of Europe Report #12462, *Inhuman treatment of people and illicit trafficking in human organs in Kosovo*, Jan. 2011. Paragraph 66 and footnote 28: The agencies dedicated to combatting drug smuggling are *"the German (BND), Italian (Sismi), British (MI6) and Greek (EYP) intelligence services"*.

[40] *Ibidem*, para. 31.

[41] *Ibid.*, para. 32.

[42] *IPS*, 'Junta's Drug Exports to China test Economic Ties', 31 Dec. 2010.

[43] Department of State, *International Narcotics Control Strategy Report volume I*, Mar. 2012, p. 144-7.

managed to place a hidden camera on one of Escobar's airplanes and obtained film of Escobar and Ministry of the Interior officials loading cocaine onto one of Escobar's planes at Managua's international airport. CBS news later broadcast the film"[44].

"Daniel Ortega and the Sandinista have regularly received money to finance FSLN electoral campaigns from international drug traffickers, usually in return for ordering Sandinista judges to allow traffickers caught by the police and military to go free"[45].

As for the neighboring Panama, his former leader and CIA informant, Manuel Noriega, ousted by the USA in 1989 was first condemned for drug trafficking and money laundering and sentenced to thirty years imprisonment in Florida, reduced to seventeen for 'good behavior'. Extradited to France, he was condemned to a seven years jail sentence for money laundering. He was extradited to Panama in December 2011.

North Korea

Pyongyang is notably accused by the U.S. government of counterfeiting its currency *"apparently done to generate foreign exchange that is used to purchase imports or finance government activities abroad*"[46].

Russia

In a 2010 widely reported U.S. diplomatic cable released by WikiLeaks, a senior Spanish prosecutor investigating organized crime *"gave a detailed, frank assessment of the activities and reach of organized crime (OC) in both Eurasia and Spain"*. For *[Belarus, Chechnya and Russia] he alleged, one cannot differentiate between the activities of the government and OC groups"*. For him Russian organized crime *"exercises 'tremendous control' over certain strategic sectors of the global economy, such as aluminum"*[47].

"[He] said that according to information he has received from intelligence services, witnesses and phone taps, certain political parties in Russia operate 'hand in hand' with OC. For example, he argued that the Liberal Democratic Party (LDP) was created by the KGB and its successor, the SVR, and is home to many serious criminals. [He] further alleged that there are proven ties between the Russian political parties, organized crime and arms trafficking. Without elaborating, he cited the strange case of the 'Artic Sea' ship in mid-2009 as 'a clear example' of arms trafficking"[48].

"He summarized his views by asserting that the [Moscow]'s strategy is to use OC groups to do whatever [it] cannot acceptably do as a government. As an example, he cited [an individual arrested in Spain], whom he said worked for Russian military intelligence to sell weapons to the Kurds to destabilize Turkey. [The Spanish prosecutor]

---

[44] Cable #63026, 5 May 2006
http://www.elpais.com/articulo/internacional/Cable/delitos/abusos/regimen/Daniel/Ortega/elpepuint/20101206elpepuint_35/Tes

[45] Cable #63040, 5 May 2006
http://www.elpais.com/articulo/internacional/Cable/jueces/sandinistas/ponen/libertad/narcos/cambio/dinero/elpepuesp/20101206elpepuint_37/Tes

[46] CRS, *North Korean Counterfeiting of U.S. currency*, 12 Jun. 2009, 15 p. and 22 mars 2006, 18 p., *International Herald tribune*, 20 Aug. 2006 'North Korea linked to Asian Banks', *Foreign policy*, Sept-Oct. 2008, p. 61.

[47] Cable #000154, 8 Feb. 2010 http://www.guardian.co.uk/world/us-embassy-cables-documents/247712

[48] *Id.*

Transnational Organized Crime—a Threat to US and International Security—Manifests Itself in Various Regions in Different Ways

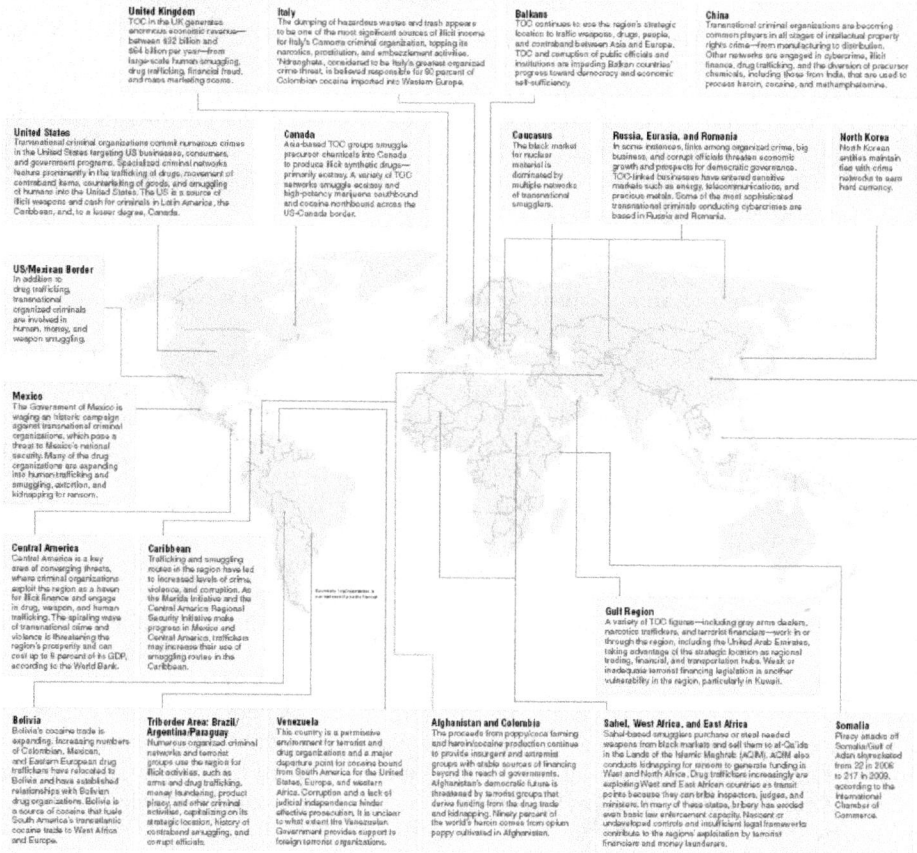

Source: U.S. Office of the Director of National Intelligence, *The threat to US national security posed by transnational organised crime*, 2011

"He summarized his views by asserting that the [Moscow]'s strategy is to use OC groups to do whatever [it] cannot acceptably do as a government. As an example, he cited [an individual arrested in Spain], whom he said worked for Russian military intelligence to sell weapons to the Kurds to destabilize Turkey. [The Spanish prosecutor] claimed that [Moscow] takes the relationship with OC leaders even further by granting them the privileges of politics, in order to grant them immunity from racketeering charges"[49].

---

[49] *Id.*

"[The Spanish prosecutor] said that he believes the FSB is 'absorbing' the Russian mafia but they can also 'eliminate' them in two ways: by killing OC leaders who do not do what the security services want them to do or by putting them behind bars to eliminate them as a competitor for influence. The crime lords can also be put in jail for their own protection"[50].

Beyond the international reaction triggered by the death of Sergueï Magnitsky, the case, 230 million dollars seemingly defrauded, allegedly with the complicity of many officials in relations with Russian organized crime would seem, if confirmed, to embody what the Spanish prosecutor described.

The illicit economy: an alternative and suppletive model of developement

Fact often misunderstood when it is simply considered, organized crime and criminal markets, just as the Cold War in the twentieth century and colonization in the nineteenth, grew to become a new geopolitical framework of the twenty-first century. They influence the evolution of society both at global and local levels as surely as the decisions taken within the G20, the World Trade Organization (WTO) or the International Monetary Fund (IMF)[51]. They also fuel a double phenomenon of politization of crime and criminalization of politics.

That is why beyond traditional divides between North and South, developed, emerging and least developed economies, a paradigm shift is probably at play whereby 'functional' states, and areas within them, are found able to limit the criminal influence below the limit of what can be considered acceptable and the others where organized crime and criminal markets represent an alternative model of development.

Consequence of the Social Pact, transition from the Behemoth to the Leviathan (Hobbes), the legitimacy of state derives from its ability to provide security, employment and reasonable prospects in climbing the social ladder. When failing to do so, the vacuum is often filled, in many areas of the world, including of course within developed countries, by criminal actors. At the end the state loses its legitimacy. This is the demise of the social Pact.

The criminal economy held up as an alternative model of development corrodes the licit sphere through corruption and the laundering of proceeds of crime. Thus organized crime and criminal markets embody a new 'invisible hand'[52]. And that is precisely the point if one wants to truly grasp the dynamic between licit and illicit economy nowadays. It is impossible to understand the effect of counterfeiting without considering the importance of this industry for some regions and states. Impossible to shed light on small arms and light weapons trafficking without considering the role played by its intermediaries, small players of greater cause. Impossible to understand the complexity of

---

[50] *Id.*

[51] Mickaël R. Roudaut, *Marchés criminels – Un acteur global*, op. cit.

[52] Mickaël R. Roudaut, *Géopolitique de l'illicite – la nouvelle main invisible*, op. cit. and *Marchés criminels – Un acteur global*. "*In economics, the* invisible hand of the market *is a metaphor to describe the self-regulating behavior of the marketplace. The idea of markets automatically channeling self-interest toward socially desirable ends is a central justification for the laissez-faire economic philosophy. In this sense, the central disagreement between economic ideologies can be viewed as a disagreement about how powerful the 'invisible hand' is*" (Wikipedia). Nowadays, organized crime, based on illicit trades economy, can play a social role thus embodies this invisible hand.

irregular migration without considering that for some economies the money sent back home, in hard currencies, from the migrants 'lucky' enough to land themselves a non-declared job in Europe or North America can represent an essential part of the local GDP, thus contributing to prevent social unrest. Impossible again to grasp the issue of grand corruption, tax evasion and money laundering without recognizing the central role played by financial opacity in the global economy...[53]

Beyond, this criminal force challenges the very foundation of modern states, based on sovereignty, since, whatever the actors or techniques, organized crime and the illegal trades their operate are transnational. Not only borders became more difficult to control due to the explosion of commercial flows but crossing them represent a great profit incentive to criminals.

Two figures in this regard. *"The value of the drugs doubles with every border crossed: a gram of heroin worth $3 in Kabul may reach $100 on the streets of London, Milan or Moscow"*[54] while one kilo of sildenafil citrate, the active ingredient of Viagra, only costs 60 dollars in South Asia. Diluted in thousands of tablets, this 60 dollar investment can be worth 300,000[55].

Thus and illustration of the polycriminal nature of transnational organised crime *"a line of cocaine snorted in Europe kills one square metre of Andean rain forest and buys one hundred rounds of AK 47 ammunition in West Africa"*[56].

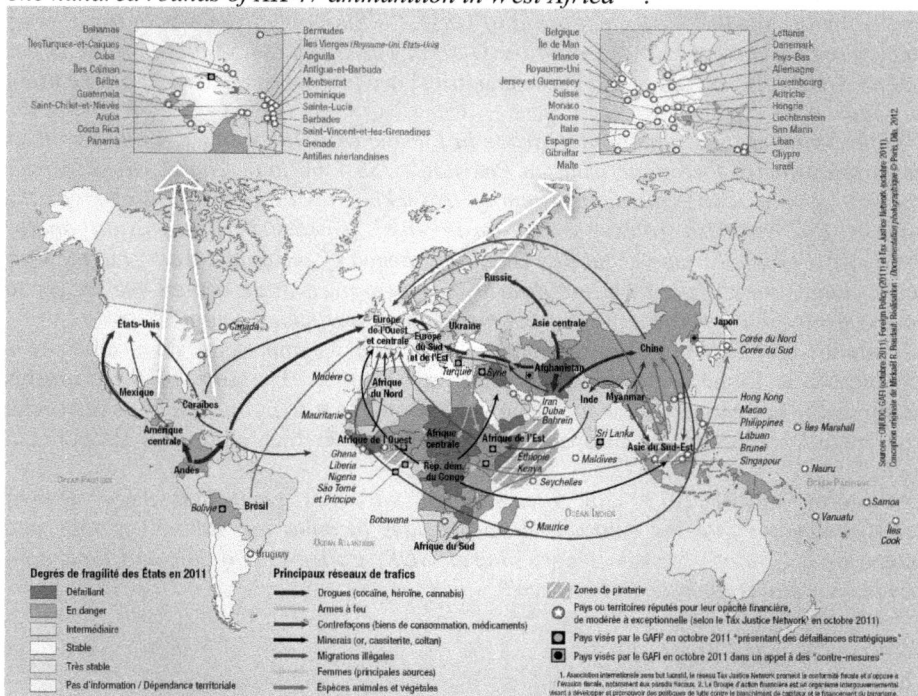

Source : Mickaël R. Roudaut, "Géopolitique de l'illicite : une nouvelle grammaire", *Géographie des conflits*

---

[53] Mickaël R. Roudaut, *Marchés criminels – Un acteur global*, op. cit.

[54] UNODC, *Addiction, crime and insurgency – The transnational threat of afghan opium*, Press release p. 2, 21 Oct. 2009.

[55] *Foreign Policy*, 'The deadly world of fake drugs', Sep-Oct. 2008, p. 61.

[56] Antonio Maria Costa then UNODC Executive Director, UN press release, 24 Feb. 2010.

Geopolitics and geoeconomics of criminal markets

Geoeconomics of drugs

The geoeconomics of drugs is well known. *"The overall value of the illicit drug market was estimated at about $320 billion for the year 2003, equivalent to 0.9 per cent of global GDP"*[57].

Of course, the heroin trade fuels both insurgency and terror. In total, the Taliban's income from the opiate trade in 2009 was around $ 155 million (ranging from 140 to 170)[58]. Beyond, *"UNODC estimates suggest that the value of Afghan traders' opiate-related sales was equivalent to slightly more than 60 per cent of the country's GDP in 2004. While this proportion decreased to 16 per cent in 2011, this figure is still very significant"*[59]. In other words, the opium trade is worth an equivalent of one sixth of the afghan 'wealth'.

Moreover, *"the total corruption cost has increased by some 40 per cent over the last three years to reach $3.9 billion"*. *"Nearly 30 per cent of Afghan citizens paid a bribe when requesting a service from individuals not employed in the public sector of Afghanistan in 2012, as opposed to the 50 per cent who paid bribes to public officials"*[60].

The invasive power of the narco-economy expands well beyond Afghan territory to follow the heroin roads. *"With a net profit of US$1.4 billion only from heroin trade, drug traffickers earned almost 31 per cent of the GDP of Tajikistan ($4.58 billion) and 33 per cent of the GDP of Kyrgyzstan*[61]. *"*[These countries] *are in a sense dependent on the illicit opiates industry"*[62].

"[T]*he value of the Afghan opiate trade in Europe (Russia excluded) is no less than 20 times the value of the opiate trade in Pakistan (US$ 1 billion). The economic power accruing to criminal organizations running trafficking operations to Europe via the Balkan or the Northern routes dwarfs insurgents' benefits in Afghanistan and/or Pakistan. As a whole, Europe's stability is not threatened by the opiate trade, but the very large revenues they extract from the drug trade have given these groups the means to achieve considerable influence in some countries along trafficking routes"*[63].

A similar link between the criminal economy and its impact on state, albeit to a lesser degree, is found concerning cannabis in Morocco. The role of the cannabis economy in the Rif Mountains is well-known. Serving as a social net, it prevents social unrest, irregular migration to Europe and Islamism, further highlighting its geopolitical influence[64].

According to the 2013 U.S. *International narcotics control strategy reports,* *"UNODC estimates that the cannabis crop provides incomes for 800,000 people, and accounts for 3.1 % of Morocco's agricultural GDP. Police corruption and tacit non-enforcement remains an issue in Morocco"*[65].

---

[57] UNODC, *World Drug Report 2012*, p. 60.

[58] UNODC, *The global afghan opium trade – A threat assessment*, Jul. 2011, p. 30.

[59] UNODC, *World drug report 2012*, p. 67.

[60] UNODC, *Corruption in Afghanistan*, Press Release, 7 Feb. 2013.

[61] UNODC, *The global afghan opium trade*, op. cit. p. 47.

[62] UNODC, *World Drug Report 2010*, p. 48.

[63] UNODC, *Addiction, crime and insurgency – The transnational threat of afghan opium*, 2009, p. 18.

[64] Alain Labrousse, *Géopolitique des drogues*, PUF, Que-sais-je? third edition, 2011, p. 38.

[65] *International Narcotics Control Strategy Report*, Vol I, Mar. 2013, p. 240.

Of course, the impact of the cannabis economy expands along the trafficking routes in Europe. Rather than referring to global figures the reader is familiar with, there is merit in mentioning the result of the 2007 French drugs observatory study on cannabis.

In France, the cannabis economy would represent 100,000 street dealers. On a monthly basis, a semi-wholesaler would earn up to 46,000 euro a month, the average salary of a manager of a company with over 2,000 employees. The first intermediate (supplier) would also benefit greatly from the cannabis economy with a monthly salary of up to 6,400 euro. The last two levels of resellers (street dealer) would only make a maximum of 800 euro per month (which could be considered as a 'cannabis minimum wage' since the minimum salary in France is roughly of 1,000 euro a month)[66].

According to a report from the organized crime intelligence and analysis department of the French police, "*criminal organizations from sensitive suburbs, responsible for massive imports of Moroccan cannabis (worth over 1 billion euro for a consumption of 250 tons a year) and continuous illegal drugs flows remain the main source of the underground economy in France*"[67].

This represents the alternative model of development previously mentioned.

Geoeconomics of counterfeiting

Counterfeiting, an industry probably claiming millions of jobs worldwide, serves as a social net within states and territories where well rooted. Tackling it would mean providing another future for these employees of the illicit. That is why its geoeconomics impact, from China to Turkey, Argentina or Morocco is generally underrated.

While the costs are difficult to quantify, and do not include non-monetary damage such as illness and death, the value of counterfeiting is estimated by the OECD to be around $250 billion a year[68]. This figure does not include domestically produced and consumed counterfeits nor digital piracy. If these were added, the total amount of counterfeiting worldwide could be several hundred billion dollars more[69].

What is the socio-economic cost of counterfeiting in Europe? Despite many reports, they tend, like a school of fish, to copy one another. The most common estimates evaluate at 200,000 the number of jobs lost each year in the EU because of counterfeiting. In France, 30,000 jobs are supposedly at stake. These figures, persistently quoted, serve as a reference. Yet, apparently not built on rigorous statistical basis nor on any comparable data, they rather reveal the absence of a more serious assessment of the social and economical consequences of the counterfeiting industry[70].

The same strategic gap has been emphasized in the USA by the Government Accountability Office (GAO – U.S. Congress). Faced with the identical issue of

---

[66] Christian Ben Lakhdar, *Le trafic de cannabis en France*, OFDT, Nov. 2007, 25 p.

[67] "*l'activisme et les capacités d'adaptation des organisations criminelles issues des cités sensibles, responsables des importations massives de cannabis marocain (plus d'un milliard d'euros pour environ 250 tonnes de résine de cannabis consommées annuellement selon la Police judiciaire) et le déploiement continu des flux de stupéfiants, demeurent la principale source d'irrigation de l'économie souterraine en France*". Le Figaro, 22 Oct. 2012.

[68] OECD, *Magnitude of counterfeiting and piracy of tangible products: an update*, Nov. 2009, p. 6.

[69] *Id.*

[70] Mickaël R. Roudaut, "From sweatshops to organized crime: the new face of counterfeiting" in *Criminal enforcement of intellectual property*, Edward Elgar publishing, Dec. 2012, p.75-95.

quantification and comparability of data, it concludes that the socio-economic impact of counterfeiting on US soil cannot be scientifically evaluated for lack of reliable data[71].

Furthermore, the more diverse counterfeiting becomes, the more it concerns products of daily use. In a causal link, the more counterfeiting attempts to penetrate official channels of distribution, and the more we all are at potential risk of buying fakes in good faith. There lies the main stake of our times. If there are many examples of penetration of official channels of distribution[72], no study evaluating this reality has however been conducted to date highlighting how unknown this criminal market remains in spite of being on everyone's lips.

Geopolitics of natural resources

The superposition of a map of civil conflicts with the cartography of natural resources in Africa presents similarities. Similarity is not causality, however in Sierra Leone, Liberia, Democratic Republic of Congo or more precisely in the Great Lakes region, or in Nigeria, the plundering of natural resources and its smuggling have played or play an important and well documented role in the financing, so in the prolongation, of these conflicts.

This is particularly the case in the Democratic Republic of Congo, where conflicts, whether declared or latent, oppose no less than six factions. Since all parties are partially if not essentially funded through natural resources, outbreaks concentrate around them. Ultimately, plundering of natural resources and civil wars feed one another.

On the long run, by contagion, it destabilizes entire regions which in turn push people to flee. Some, choosing exile in Europe, employ the services of criminal networks since Europol views irregular migration to the EU as being essentially facilitated to one degree or another by organized crime.

Once in Europe, many of them, when asylum is not granted, can become irregular workers on construction sites, sell counterfeit, others (mostly women) can be coerced in prostitution rings illustrating the symbiotic links between irregular migration, trafficking in persons, non-declared labour and violations of intellectual property rights, all this also impacting on the legal economy[73].

Geoeconomics of irregular migration

The lack of political will sometimes deplored in Europe or North America from the emigration states in the fight against irregular migration networks exploiting their nationals could find its origin in the following.

Not only candidates to exile mainly consist of 'left behind' within disfranchised communities who, in lack of emigration prospects could fuel social unrest (food riots...) but turning a blind eye on these criminal rings, allows emigration countries to benefit from a means of economic development through remittances provided to family members who remained behind. Some of these countries heavily depend on this hard currency flow sometimes representing a third of their GDP. Ultimately, they are simply subsidized by their migrants[74] illustrating how irregular migration can be necessary to their viability.

---

[71] United States Government Accountability Office, *Observations on Efforts to Quantify the Economic Effects of Counterfeit and Pirated Goods*, Apr. 2010, p. 37.

[72] Mickaël R. Roudaut, *From sweatshops to organized crime: the new face of counterfeiting*, op. cit.

[73] Mickaël R. Roudaut, *Marchés criminels – Un acteur global*, op. cit. and *Géopolitique de l'illicite – la nouvelle main invisible*, op. cit.

[74] *Id.*

Financial opacity: the bridge between licit and illicit economy

Illegal trades are big business. The UNODC suggests that all criminal proceeds, excluding tax evasion, would amount to some 2.1 trillion dollars in 2009. Out of this total, the proceeds of transnational organized crime would be considered of 1.5 % of the global GDP, 70 % of which would likely have been laundered through the financial system[75].

In our times, a 'successful' state does not only require the harmonious superposition of a Nation over a territory. It must also be economically sustainable; hence the temptation of some territories and states to trade their sovereignty in order to attract the necessary capital ensuring their development. Tax evasion, money laundering and grand corruption benefit from the financial opacity then organized which in turn distorts the global economy[76].

What to conclude from recent events? According to the audit from FINMA, the Swiss Financial Market Supervisory Authority, conducted as part of the identification of the assets held by the three Arab leaders ousted, four of the 20 Swiss banks examined were not following, sometimes crudely, prudential rules in their relationships with 'politically exposed persons' (head of State, ambassadors, heads of public enterprises, members of their families...).

Les plus grosses amendes pour blanchiment d'argent
En millions de dollars

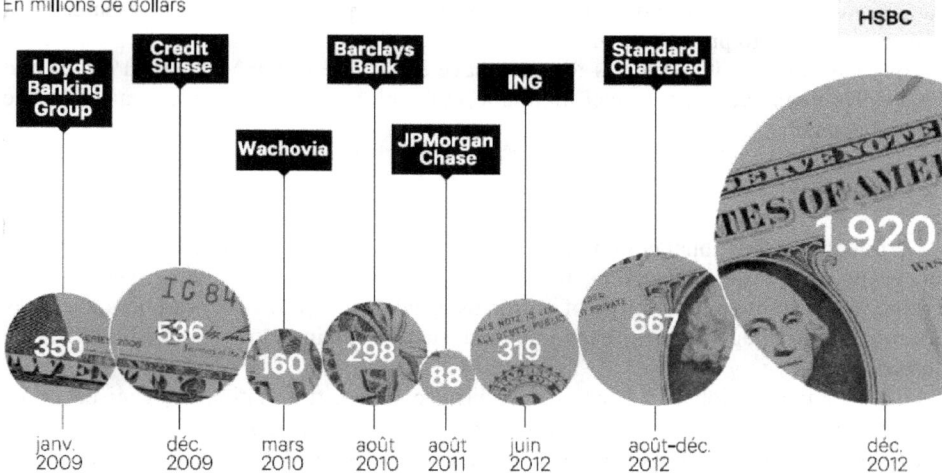

HSBC							
Lloyds Banking Group	Credit Suisse		Barclays Bank		ING	Standard Chartered	
		Wachovia		JPMorgan Chase			
350	536	160	298	88	319	667	1.920
janv. 2009	déc. 2009	mars 2010	août 2010	août 2011	juin 2012	août-déc. 2012	déc. 2012

«LES ÉCHOS» / PHOTO : DR

'The biggest money laundering fines in millions of dollars'
Source: *Les Echos,* 12 Dec. 2012

A similar audit conducted by the FSA, the UK Financial Services Authority stated *"Serious weaknesses identified in banks' systems and controls, as well as indications that some banks are willing to enter into very high-risk business relationships without adequate controls when there are potentially large profits to be made, means that it is*

---

[75] UNODC, *Estimating illicit financial flows resulting from drug trafficking and other transnational organized crime,* Press release, 25 Oct. 2011.
[76] Mickaël R. Roudaut, *Géopolitique de la crise, des monnaies et de la fraude,* op. cit.

likely that some banks are handling the proceeds of corruption or other financial crime"[77].

Ultimately, the recent cases of Wachovia, Sal-LCB banks, Standard Chartered, Crédit Suisse, or HSBC are only the consequences of a larger reality, licit and illicit finances, far from excluding one another, responding to the law of supply and demand tend to attract each other.

This is where the opacity organized by some states and territories creates a bridge between legal and illicit economies. This bridge, this service, is used for tax evasion, grand corruption and money laundering alike.

Of course, this leads to further increase the tax burden on fair tax payers contributing for the others. In emerging countries, this contributes to widen the gap between rich and poor. This also has an impact on the euro zone crisis.

In its 2011 report, Transparency International sees in the economic difficulties of the euro zone the "*inability of the government to fight against corruption and tax evasion. In Germany and France, official estimates of losses due tax fraud are around 30 billion euro a year, which represent a third of their respective annual deficit. In comparison, in countries where tax evasion is seen as endemic and the most hit by the euro financial crisis, the amount of revenue loss is of the same magnitude as the amount of the annual deficit*"[78].

If fraud and tax evasion are of course not the 'only explanation' to the crisis in the euro zone, they are a cause of its lasting effect. That is why one of the keys to the fight against money laundering, tax evasion and grand corruption lies in the transparency of legal entities so as to prevent them from being a vehicle to fraud[79].

Beyond, money laundering is found to have had a role in the Mexican (1994-5) and Thai (1997) financial crisis, further highlighting the global stability concern raised by the criminal economy[80].

Conclusion

While the international community concerns tend to remain focused around terrorism and weapons of mass destruction, the illicit economy became an alternative model of development attracting a new type of criminals, state. Yet, by lack of awareness, the links between crime, illegal trades, economy and states remain poorly studied and rarely debated[81]

Even though a global and national security concern, transnational organised crime and illegal trades remain too often confined to a law enforcement issue. Clearly, there is a need to fundamentally rethink the way organized crime is defined and understood.

---

[77] FSA, *Banks' management of high money-laundering risk situations*, Jun. 2011, 94 p. spéc. p. 6.
[78] *Le Monde,* 1st Dec. 2011.
[79] Michael Findley, Daniel Nielson and Jason Sharman, *Global Shell Games: Testing Money Launderers' and Terrorist Financiers' Access to Shell Companies*, 2012, 33 p. and World Bank, *The puppet Masters*, 284 p. Oct. 2011.
[80] Guilhem Favre, 'Prospering on crime: Money laundering and Financial Crisis', 2005, *Centre for East and South-East Asian Studies.*
[81] A welcome initiative, the OECD launched in 2012 new activities aiming to quantify the impacts of illegal trades and the illegal economy on economic growth, sustainable development and global security.

About the author
Mickaël R. Roudaut is notably author of *Marchés criminels – Un acteur global* (2010), Presses Universitaires de France, Paris. He lectures at the Universities of Paris II Panthéon-Assas, Clermont-Ferrand and at the *Gendarmerie nationale* Officers academy.

www.ingramcontent.com/pod-product-compliance
Lightning Source LLC
Chambersburg PA
CBHW081657270326
41933CB00017B/3194